INTRODUCTION TO EMPTINESS

Introduction to Emptiness

AS TAUGHT IN TSONG-KHA-PA'S

Great Treatise on the
Stages of the Path

Guy Newland

SNOW LION | BOSTON & LONDON

Snow Lion
An imprint of Shambhala Publications, Inc.
Horticultural Hall
300 Massachusetts Avenue
Boston, Massachusetts 02115
www.shambhala.com

An excerpt (on p. v) from the lyrics of "Making Flippy Floppy,"
published by Index Music, Inc., is used by permission of David
Byrne. "The Old Man Said: One" (on p. v) from Carroll Arnett's *Night
Perimeter* (Greenfield Review Press) is used by permission of his estate.

9 8 7 6 5 4 3

Printed in the United States of America

♾ This edition is printed on acid-free paper that meets
the American National Standards Institute z39.48 Standard.
♻ Shambhala Publications makes every effort to print on recycled
paper. For more information please visit www.shambhala.com.
Distributed in the United States by Random House, Inc.,
and in Canada by Random House of Canada Ltd

Designed and typeset by Gopa & Ted2, Inc.

Library of Congress Cataloging-in-Publication Data

Newland, Guy.
Introduction to emptiness : as taught in Tsong-kha-pa's Great treatise
on the stages of the path / Guy Newland. — 2nd ed.
p. cm.
Includes bibliographical references.
ISBN 978-1-55939-332-4 (alk. paper)
1. Tsoṅ-kha-pa Blo-bzaṅ-grags-pa, 1357–1419. Lam rim chen mo.
2. Lam-rim. 3. Sunyata. 4. Mādhyamika (Buddhism) I. Title.
BQ7950.T754L344436 2009
294.3'422—dc22
2009023597

Ev'rything is divided
Nothing is complete
Ev'rything looks impressive
Do not be deceived
—DAVID BYRNE

Some will tell
you it doesn't
matter. That is
a lie. Everything,
every single thing
matters. And
nothing good
happens fast.
—GOGISGI (CARROLL ARNETT)

Contents

Introduction

EMPTINESS? We know that Buddhism teaches that the ultimate reality is emptiness, so it must be important. Perhaps we feel that the word hints at some sort of mystical nothingness. Understanding emptiness has always been something of a challenge, even when we have strong motivation. I hope that this book will help.

If you are a person with some background in Buddhism but without specialized expertise in Buddhist philosophy, then—whether you are a serious practitioner or just curious—I have written with you in mind. I am eager to introduce you to something that has been my abiding fascination for more than thirty years: emptiness as presented in the Ge-luk sect of Tibetan Buddhism.

I wrote this book mainly by summarizing and explaining in my own words key ideas and arguments that the sect's founder, Tsong-kha-pa Lo-sang-drak-pa (1357–1419), puts forward in the "insight" section of his massive text *The Great Treatise on the Stages of the Path* (*byang chub lam rim chen mo*; *Great Treatise* hereafter). Tsong-kha-pa had mastered the literature of Indian and Tibetan Buddhism that he had inherited. After extensive meditation, he arrived at a brilliant and comprehensive vision synthesizing and reconciling the meanings of these teachings. In 1402, Tsong-kha-pa presented this vision in the *Great Treatise*; six hundred years later, Joshua Cutler led a group of Buddhist scholars in publishing a complete translation into English (Snow Lion Publications, 2000–2004). When making reference to the *Great Treatise* in this book, I have cited this translation by volume number and page number.

As Joshua and I edited this work, we really wanted to create a translation that was faithful to the Tibetan but also clear and readable in English. We think that in most parts we were able to achieve this goal, but some portions of Volume Three—dealing with *insight* into emptiness as the fundamental nature of reality—are of such complexity that no translation can, in itself, make them completely accessible to the general reader. This is simply because, like most traditional Buddhist writers, when Tsong-kha-pa wrote about emptiness he was not setting out to make it clear to beginners.

My goal in this book is to bridge the gap between contemporary readers who would like to understand emptiness and Tsong-kha-pa's profound explanations. Because the *Great Treatise* is indisputably a classic work, it is certain that there will be other books to help readers aspiring to delve deeply into even the thorniest portions of the insight section. For now, we need a place to start. I have aimed to provide access to some of its meaning by distilling, summarizing, and restating Tsong-kha-pa's key ideas using the same examples I use with my own students. Inspired by the Tibetan literary tradition, I have further identified the quintessential points within this presentation; these appear as an appendix to the book.

Anyone who reads Tsong-kha-pa closely will feel the power of the inspiration that touched him. His teachings have universal appeal, clarifying much in the texture of daily, human experience in any century. The door of this teaching should be wide open to all who feel drawn to meet the challenge.

Acknowledgments

THE IDEAS HERE are those of Tsong-kha-pa. In finding ways to distill and represent these ideas I was particularly aided by the published works of Elizabeth Napper and Jeffrey Hopkins, especially Napper's *Dependent-Arising and Emptiness* (Wisdom Publications, 1989) and "Ethics as the Basis of a Tantric Tradition" in *Changing Minds* (Snow Lion Publications, 2001) along with Hopkins's *Meditation on Emptiness* (Wisdom Publications, 1983), *Emptiness Yoga* (Snow Lion Publications, 1987) and "A Tibetan Delineation of Different Views of Emptiness in the Middle Way School" (in *Tibet Journal* 14, no. 1 [1989]).

Study with Geshe Palden Drakpa and Gen Losang Gyatso in India prepared me to conceptualize and to express Tsong-kha-pa's teachings. Geshe Palden Drakpa tuned in to my questions and, with great compassion, extended himself to give me clues that I needed to understand something of the Madhyamaka system. Some of these clues led me directly to the *Great Treatise*.

I also thank Donald S. Lopez, Jr., who was my first Tibetan instructor and also the person who conceived of the Lamrim Chenmo translation project. I have been further aided in my thinking about emptiness over the years by connections with many others, including Jay Garfield, William Magee, Anne Klein, Dan Cozort, Georges Dreyfus, and David Loy.

In attempting to write about emptiness while minimizing the scholastic jargon, I am inspired by diverse authors and teachers who have done this before, including Jeffrey Hopkins in *The Tantric Distinction* (Wisdom Publications, 1984), Paul Williams in "Madhyamaka for Midwives" (in *The Middle Way* 66 [1992]), Bob Thurman, David Loy, Roger Corless, Robert Aitken, Gary Snyder, Thich Nhat Hanh, Shunryu Suzuki, Lama Yeshe, Kensur Lekden, Geshe Rabten, and His Holiness the Dalai Lama Tenzin Gyatso. I also thank those students at Central Michigan University who—because they genuinely wanted to understand—asked me to explain emptiness again, in another way.

Special thanks to Thubten Chodron and Sidney Piburn for invaluable comments on the manuscript. Thanks also to Kai Mummenbrauer for his corrections, to Michael Wakoff and Steve Rhodes for their editing work, and to Gabriel Newland for helpful suggestions.

I thank my wife, Valerie Stephens, for her love and support.

The heart of this work arises from the fierce Dharma spirit of Diana Cutler. Along with Joshua, she inspired me in the beginning and along the way provided the encouragement and financial support I needed. This book would not exist without her. I dedicate it to Geshe Ngawang Wangyal and to our compassionate teacher, His Holiness the Dalai Lama.

1. How to Be Free*

Empty as the Sky

WE SUFFER UNNECESSARILY because we do not know ourselves. Like addicts fiercely clinging to a drug, we cannot let go of the sense that we are substantial, solid, independent, and autonomous. We lay schemes large and small to acquire and to harm—all grounded in this false apprehension of how we exist, who we are as living beings. On behalf of this exaggerated self, with fear, anger, and pride, we harm others. To nurture and to satisfy each passing whim of this exaggerated self, we build up our greed. Yet the path of greed and harm does not at all lead us toward happiness; it is samsara, the cyclic path of dissatisfaction and misery. Over and over again, moment after moment, we fall into this trap we have unwittingly built for ourselves. Like an addict's drug, the false notion of an independently existing self is the source of great misery for ourselves and others.

Of course, we do exist. We are living beings. We make choices and our choices make a difference, for ourselves and others. But at some level, for all of us, we cannot just leave it at that. To be real, to be alive, we feel that we must deep down somehow exist in a solid and independent way. Death tells us a very different story, but for that very reason we find a million ways to avoid hearing the message of death. That message is that we are impermanent. Our bodies are disintegrating moment by moment, right now. And though

---

* This chapter is based mainly on the *Great Treatise*, Volume 2.

we desperately wish to believe otherwise, the truth is that beneath our ever-changing minds and aging bodies there is no eternal and essential self. We have no natural existence, no independent way of existing.

We exist contingently, interdependently. We exist, but only in dependence on our ancestors, our body parts, our food, air, and water, and the other members of our society. We could not and do not exist otherwise. Devoid of any independent or substantial nature, our existence is possible only because it is far less rigid, less concrete, than what we imagine it to be.

Rather than seeing things as they are, we superimpose upon ourselves—and on things around us—a false existence, a self-existence or essential reality that actually does not exist at all. In the Buddhist philosophy explained here, the ultimate truth is the sheer absence, the lack, of any such essence. This is emptiness (*stong pa nyid*, *shunyata*). While this may sound bleak, disappointing, or frightening, it is the very nature of reality. And it is reality—not fantasy—that is our final hope and our refuge. The path to freedom from needless misery, for ourselves and others, is through profound realization of this fundamental reality.

As we begin, how can we feel that "emptiness" is such a positive thing? The word has powerful negative connotations. It suggests, at first, quite the opposite of a liberating spiritual path. It may suggest hollowness, deadness, despair, and hopelessness. It may suggest meaninglessness. If we listen to how the word resonates through our associations, it seems even to suggest that nothing matters at all.

The Tibetan and Sanskrit words that we translate as "emptiness" do, in fact, literally mean "emptiness." They refer specifically to some sort of lack or absence in things. But it is not a lack of meaning or hope or existence. It is the lack of the exaggerated and distorted kind of existence that we have projected onto things and onto ourselves. It is the absence of a false essential nature with which we have unconsciously invested everything. It can be quite frightening as we start to have doubts about this "heavy duty" kind of reality. We will feel that things cannot exist at all if they do not exist in the solid way we are accustomed to seeing them.

Consider, however, that if we actually did have a very solid kind of existence, it would mean that we could *never* change. If it were our essential nature to be as we are, we would always be exactly that. We would be locked into existence-just-as-what-we-are-now. There could be no life—everything would be static and frozen. We could not interact with other living beings, growing and learning. How could we become wiser? How would we find happiness?

As we live and grow, we learn that we are happy when we can bring happiness to others. Other living beings, and their suffering, are empty, but this does not at all negate their existence or the painfulness of their suffering. Instead, it means that this suffering is not a fixed part of reality—it can be changed. In fact, it *will* change, but whether it gets better or worse depends on causes and conditions—which means that, in part, it depends on us.

We can think of emptiness as like the clear, blue sky—a transparent space that is wide open.[1] In that way, our empty natures mean that there is no limit to what we can become. We are not blocked, obstructed, or tied down. Right now, our powers to help others may be limited, but emptiness is the lack of chains preventing us from becoming more wise and loving. It is the absence of bars on the door, the freedom from any built-in limit on what we can be. How wise can we become? How loving? When we wonder about this, let's not impose limitations that are not part of reality.

Inevitably we face difficulties—sometimes great difficulties. The path demands time and effort. But the obstacles are not insurmountable because they are not intrinsic to the structure of reality. Fundamentally, all things are empty—and so we are empty—of any intrinsic nature. This is why the reality of emptiness, properly understood, is a tremendous wellspring of hope and inspiration. Only because we are empty, the possibilities for what we can become are wide open. The sky is the limit.

Tsong-kha-pa's Teaching

In this book I will summarize how Tsong-kha-pa Lo-sang-drak-pa, founder of the Ge-luk order of Tibetan Buddhism, explains emptiness in the latter portions of *The Great Treatise on the Stages of the Path* (*Great Treatise* hereafter). Published in 1402, the *Great Treatise* was the first of five major works in which Tsong-kha-pa expounded his approach to Buddhist philosophy, an approach in which the validity of logic and ethical norms is maintained within a radical view of emptiness—the view that all phenomena are devoid of any essential or intrinsic nature. Like other Mahayana Buddhists, Tsong-kha-pa believes that all living beings have the potential to attain perfect happiness as fully enlightened buddhas. The spiritual path to buddhahood involves balanced development of two factors: wisdom—which knows the emptiness of all that exists— and compassionate action for the welfare of other living beings. Wisdom destroys all reification and penetrates ultimate truth, while leaving intact the conventional truths that allow us to exist, to make ethical distinctions, and to help those who suffer.

The root of our current unsatisfactory condition in a cycle of death and rebirth is our innate tendency to hold a distorted, reifying view of ourselves; we also have innate tendencies to view all other phenomena in the same manner. To achieve wisdom, to know emptiness, is to overcome this reifying view by seeing that the exaggerated self we have imagined does not in fact exist at all. In order to reach this realization, Tsong-kha-pa stressed, we have to use reason to refute the existence—to prove the nonexistence— of this reified self or essence.

Our utter lack of a self-existent self—an independently existing self, an ultimately real self—does *not* mean that we do not exist at all. Persons and other phenomena do exist interdependently. The Buddha spoke of "himself" and his actions. He used the word "I." It is natural and correct to use language this way. Persons and other things exist only in a conventional sense, but existing in just this way is fully sufficient—and in fact necessary—for them to function as they do. Without any fixed, unchanging, intrinsic nature—without any intrinsic capacity to exist—we are nonetheless fully capable of choosing and acting.

Having arrived through analytical introspection at the correct philosophical view—that the self lacks a shred of intrinsic nature—a bodhisattva, in quest of buddhahood, proceeds along the path through intense, deep, and extensive meditative familiarization with this view. These wisdom practices operate in a powerful synergy with the bodhisattva's compassion and love.

Some may see it as paradoxical or even absurd that bodhisattvas develop powerful compassion for beings whose fundamental nature is emptiness. But in practice, realizing emptiness can support and augment the power of compassion in a number of ways. (1) By seeing that there is no inherently existent difference between self and other, the meditator undermines his self-cherishing sense of "looking out for number one." He no longer believes that there is an independently existing self "over here" that ought to be protected and satisfied to the exclusion of, or even at the expense of, all of those essentially other persons "out there." (2) Also, by seeing that she shares with all beings a fundamental nature of emptiness, the meditator strengthens the deep sense of closeness and relatedness to others that is critical to her love and compassion. (3) In order to aspire to attain buddhahood for the sake of all beings, and knowing that the state of being a buddha is radically different from his current condition, the meditator needs to develop a powerful conviction that it is actually possible to become so transformed as to become a fully enlightened buddha. This conviction grows out of an understanding that his present, limited capacity to help others is not inherent in his very nature. His fundamental nature is pure emptiness, opening up endless possibilities for transformation. (4) When a bodhisattva trains in compassion-motivated practices such as generosity, her virtues are purified and qualified as *perfections* through being associated with the bodhisattva's wisdom understanding that giver, gift, recipient, and the very act of giving itself are all devoid of any inherent existence.

The Power of Wisdom

Committed to bringing happiness to all beings, a bodhisattva from the outset seeks to attain the enormous helping powers of a buddha by training in the six perfections:

- generosity
- ethical discipline
- patience
- joyous perseverance
- meditative stabilization
- wisdom

The idea is first to cultivate each of these virtues and then to practice them in such a way that each is imbued with and supported by the latent power of the others. Generosity is the mental inclination to share material resources with others, to protect them, and to teach them the Dharma. Ethical discipline is letting go of thoughts and tendencies to harm others. Patience is disregarding harm done to you by others, courageously accepting your own suffering, and maintaining a faithful conviction in the Dharma. Joyous perseverance is enthusiasm and joyful energy that enables us to be steadfast in virtuous activity.

Meditative stabilization is a virtuous consciousness that stays fixed on its object of meditation without distraction to other things. This powerful and stable type of mind is a wonderful tool, an "inner technology" that can be used for many purposes.

Wisdom has a range of meanings. It often refers very specifically to a consciousness that powerfully discerns ultimate reality, how things exist in the final analysis. This most particular sort of wisdom, a mind that knows emptiness, is our primary concern in this book. Such a mind comprehends that things are empty in the sense that they lack any existence in and of themselves. Things exist, but only in dependence upon one another.

In a broader sense, however, wisdom is any instance of discerning and analytical understanding that can sort out "what is what," seeing things for what they are. Tsong-kha-pa teaches that this sort of discerning wisdom is absolutely critical to the path. The way to begin to develop wisdom—or any virtue—is to reflect on the benefits of having it and the faults of not having it. Difficulties will arise in any endeavor, so it is important to prepare ourselves by first considering carefully the goal we are trying to achieve. When the reasons for aspiring to this goal are set very clearly in our minds, then we are armored against discouragement.

In fact, this kind of discerning understanding—sorting out what is good about wisdom and what is bad about lacking it—is already a sort of wisdom. Wisdom is like our spiritual vision, guiding us toward what is good. Its guiding role among the six perfections is compared to the role of the mental consciousness in relation to the five senses. It is wisdom that enables bodhisattvas to make sound decisions about what to do and what not to do.

For example, consider the first perfection, generosity. In the case of someone just beginning to practice generosity, it is wisdom that understands the advantages of generosity and the faults of stinginess. Later, for advanced bodhisattvas, it is nondualistic wisdom directly penetrating emptiness—ultimate reality—that allows them to practice more radical and powerful types of generosity (which would otherwise be highly inadvisable) such as giving away even their own flesh to those who need it.

Lacking the wisdom to make very careful distinctions, we are strongly disposed simply to accept things as they appear on the surface. This is a profound fault that causes inconceivably vast amounts of unnecessary misery. A hungry pizza-lover may see a pizza as something radiant, glowing from within with natural goodness. While not actually thinking this consciously, the pizza-lover accepts this appearance and reacts to the pizza as though it were a natural source of happiness in and of itself. Yet a short while later he may have a burned mouth and some garbage to dispose of.

Take another example: Suppose a man cuts in front of me in a long line at the bank—I might assume that this person is bad and deserves a stern rebuke or worse. I may well see the man as a naturally bad person and his action as a simple expression of this bad nature. Even if I restrain my speech and action, my mind is in a tumult of righteous anger. I may feel that the person deserves to be smacked, even though I am too virtuous a person to carry out the smacking. At that time, the person appears to my mind as intrinsically bad, naturally and objectively deserving of smacking. My violent feelings and sense of righteousness are based on an unexamined assumption that the man was intentionally harming me and had no legitimate reason for stepping in front of me.

But what if I am wrong? Perhaps I should investigate, asking a polite question rather than seething. And even if the line-cutting man did cut me off intentionally, perhaps this is an aberrant behavior caused by a temporary mental disturbance. Why is it hard to distinguish between a person who happens to be acting rudely toward me and a person who is my enemy because of being fundamentally, essentially, permanently one who is there to hurt me? Wisdom teaches us that our real enemies are never other living beings. They are ignorance and its minions, including greed, hatred, anger, pride, and envy.

Things often appear to our minds as though they were independent and unchanging—but they are actually contingent upon myriad conditions and changing constantly, instant by instant. As the conditions they depend on change, they rot, break, and disintegrate altogether. Without stopping to investigate, we all tend to accept things as they superficially appear. These false appearances are fueled by our pride, anger, and desire, and at the same time they arise in ways that stoke these fires higher. For example, believing that our human foes are naturally evil and our friends are naturally good—just as they appear in our minds—we set out for war with the absolute, dead certainty that our violent actions are moral, just, noble—perhaps even holy.

There are other ways that not having wisdom causes us problems. Through failing to analyze carefully, we tend to treat as though absolutely contradictory and mutually exclusive many things that are in fact only superficially discordant, or that occur together infrequently. Tsong-kha-pa teaches us that careful discernment is one of the most important aspects of wisdom. This theme runs throughout the *Great Treatise*. For example, we might think that intense affection contradicts nonattachment, but—guided by wisdom—bodhisattvas can have very strong love for all living beings without a trace of attachment. Or, we may feel that discouragement would be inevitable as we become sensitized to the intolerable torment in which so many beings live, but for bodhisattvas guided by wisdom this is not so. Again, bodhisattvas can have a sense of infinite joy and bliss without any "giddiness" or mental instability—and it is wisdom that makes possible this balancing act.

There are also many passages in Buddhist scriptures that seem contradictory. For example, there are differences between the vows taught in the Mahayana sutras and those that appear in Buddhist tantric texts. Without the light of wisdom to guide us to the intended meaning of such passages, we easily fall into a tangle of unending confusion as to how to proceed.

A particularly important case in which only clear wisdom can discern compatibility is the case of ultimate reality and conventional existence. Many Buddhists and non-Buddhists have reached the conclusion that profound emptiness—that all things lack even a shred of intrinsic nature—is incompatible with conventional existence in which specific effects arise in dependence upon their respective causes and conditions. Once you adopt this error, you have a limited number of choices: You can believe in emptiness while treating as polite fictions the conventional existence of people, distinctions between right and wrong, etc. Or you can believe in the reality of things just as they appear and discard the profound wisdom of Buddhism. Or else you can discard all reason and insist that emptiness and conventional cause-effect relationships are both valid, even though completely contradictory. Wisdom that is sharp, patient, and discerning will see that all of these choices are bad and unnecessary. In the *Great Treatise*, Tsong-kha-pa sets out to prove this and to chart the alternative.

How to Become Wise

All good qualities arise from wisdom, so we should do everything we can to develop and strengthen this quality. Antithetical to the clarity of wisdom is confusion, which arises from conditions such as keeping bad company, laziness, incuriosity, distaste for analysis, thinking you already know things and thus do not have to study or analyze, being influenced by wrong philosophical views, and from thoughts such as, "Someone like me could never understand this."

An indispensable key to developing wisdom is *studying* the Dharma to the very best of our abilities. Broad study of Buddhist scriptures and their commentaries is, according to Tsong-kha-pa, the "sacred life force of the path." By reflecting on what you have learned through study, you internalize the teachings, taking the Dharma to heart. It is precisely these very teachings—not some different instruction whispered by a spiritual teacher—that you then take up in meditation. Thus, while some Buddhists make a distinction between great scholars (discursive) and great meditators (nondiscursive), leaving broad study for the former, Tsong-kha-pa shows that it is precisely those setting out to meditate seriously who most need to study the teachings carefully so as to avoid going astray in their meditation practice. It is spiritual poison to believe that serious practice can bypass study and discerning analysis. How can we practice something or meditate on something that we have never taken the trouble to understand?

The best way to uphold the Dharma is to practice it correctly; to practice correctly we need to study scriptures so as to understand what the Buddha taught. Listen to the teachings and take them as personal advice for practice. When setting out to study Buddhist texts, their breadth, complexity, and internal differences may sometimes be daunting, but we should do the best we can with the analytical capacity we have. Remember that study and practice are not different things. Your meditation practice must be exactly what you have first studied and thought about carefully. When you understand something and have taken it to heart, then it can serve as a beneficial focal point for deep meditation.

The Source of All Virtue

Buddhist texts teach that everything good, in this world and beyond, derives from serenity and insight. As we will see, serenity and insight are special meditative qualities that a spiritual practitioner develops only after long training; they are well-developed forms of the fifth and sixth perfections—meditative stabilization and wisdom. This raises a question: How can all virtue derive from something that most Buddhists have yet to attain? Tsongkha-pa explains that these passages are not to be read in such a narrow sense. In this case "serenity" broadly includes all minds that focus one-pointedly on a virtuous object and "insight" carries the broad sense of discerning attention to facts. Thus, these teachings mean that whether we consider ourselves, the buddhas, or anyone in between, *all virtue everywhere can be traced back to the mental practice of reflecting on facts with an undistracted mind.*

Buddhist teachings include a truly vast number of different meditation techniques, but they can be summed up within the categories pertaining to serenity and insight: (1) meditations that engage and strengthen our capacity to focus and to stabilize the mind without distraction—culminating in perfect serenity, and (2) meditations that use and develop the capacity to discern and to analyze the qualities of an object—culminating in meditative wisdom, or insight. The full benefits of Buddhist meditation come only through a balanced practice in which both of these capacities are fully developed; neither analytical meditation nor stabilizing meditation alone can suffice.

The reason for this is that our problems, our mental afflictions, exist in both active and latent forms. We are regularly afflicted by painful eruptions of greed, hatred, jealousy, fear, anger, pride, and delusion. Yet even when such afflictions do not manifest themselves so forcefully, or seem altogether absent, we remain deeply predisposed to them. They are latent, hidden like roots deep in our mind-streams. Meditative serenity suppresses the disturbing and painful manifest forms of the afflictions, the weeds on the surface of the mind. This creates a clear field within which meditative wisdom can develop into profound insight, penetrating through subtler and subtler levels of self-deception so as eventually to root out even the subtlest latent forms of the afflictions.

2. Following the Path of Wisdom*

An Overview

To MEDITATE ON emptiness, we must first identify our own most fundamental misconceptions. Through careful practice with a teacher, meditators can learn to locate within their own experience the particular sense of self that is the deepest root of cyclic misery. Once the meditator introspectively locates very precisely the target conception of self, she uses logical analysis in meditation to see whether such a self could actually exist as it appears. Using reason to prove that it does not and could not exist, she realizes emptiness.

This knowledge of emptiness, the ultimate reality of all things, is a profound certainty attained through introspective meditation and inferential reasoning. It is transformative to know with certainty that things do not exist as they have been appearing to one's mind. However, it is still a conceptual and therefore a dualistic kind of understanding. Nirvana, the actual experience of liberating insight, is a direct and nondualistic perception of emptiness. In order to refine a powerful but conceptual understanding of emptiness into direct, nondualistic experience, the bodhisattva uses the power of concentration meditation, meditative stabilization.

Concentration is a state in which the mind rests upon its object one-pointedly and without any distraction. When one is concentrated upon an object, the dualistic sense of subject and object

---

* Based mainly on the *Great Treatise*, Volume 3, Chapters 7–9.

fades. The subtle, pervasive feeling that "I am over here and my object is over there" is diluted more and more by the power of concentration. One becomes, as we say, utterly *absorbed* in one's object of concentration, losing all sense of time and self-consciousness. Strengthening their analysis of emptiness with the power of concentration, bodhisattvas gradually develop deep *insight* into emptiness. Through the practice of insight, their experience of emptiness becomes less conceptual and less dualistic. Finally, they are able to know emptiness directly and nonconceptually. This is nirvana, the actual antidote or "active ingredient" in the medicine of the Dharma. A single, direct, nondualistic realization of emptiness eradicates permanently some portion of the desire, hatred, and ignorance that have bound one in misery for infinite cycles of time up until that moment. Repeated realizations over many lifetimes are still needed before all of the ancient roots of ignorance can be eradicated. During this training, the bodhisattva alternates between periods of meditation on emptiness and periods of compassionate action in the world. Even after the bodhisattva escapes samsara altogether, she must still practice for a long time to overcome the "hangover" of dualistic appearances, the aftereffects of having been ignorant for so long. Finally, these last limitations are cleared away and the bodhisattva becomes a buddha. A buddha continuously knows emptiness directly while also simultaneously acting compassionately in the world of persons and forms.

Wisdom as the Unique Power of the Buddhist Path

The Buddhist path is often summarized as three trainings: training in ethics, training in meditative stabilization, and training in wisdom. The training in ethics includes practices such as restraining violent actions, restraining abusive speech, and restraining even thoughts of harming others. The training in ethics also extends to practices that develop kindness and love along with powerful altruistic motivations.

The training in meditative stabilization involves systematically calming and focusing one's mind until, with perfect clarity, it will remain in focused attention on any object to which one turns. Meditative stabilizations are powerful and blissful consciousnesses, some of which are said to make the meditator capable of supernormal feats.

While these first two trainings are crucial to the path, it is also true that many non-Buddhist traditions share with Buddhism important practices and ideals such as these. That is, a great many religions teach their followers to be hospitable, kind, considerate, empathetic—even loving. Some religions share with Buddhism the teaching that we should love and seek happiness even for those who harm us.

Likewise, many non-Buddhist traditions have practices for calming and focusing the mind. The traditional story of Siddhartha's life tells us that he mastered techniques of meditative stabilization as taught by non-Buddhist teachers (Udraka and Arada Kalama) well before he found the middle way and attained enlightenment. When one goes into a deeply concentrated state of meditative stabilization, one is free for that time from ordinary, mundane troubles. But eventually, like a vacation to the beach, one's meditation must end, and upon returning to the world one is faced again with the same problems. One is not necessarily any wiser or any more skillful in coping or in helping others.

As the suffering world has no independent, objective reality but is only an empty convention, we might suppose that stopping conventional thought in a meditative state would be the most liberating move. The Chinese Buddhist master Ha-shang Mahayana, Tsong-kha-pa reports, regarded any sort of conceptualization whatsoever to be a distorting reification. Throughout the *Great Treatise*, Ha-shang functions as a stock character representing the perspective that we should dispense with all thought and meditate on reality by not bringing anything to mind.

Tsong-kha-pa argues repeatedly and passionately that meditative thoughtlessness is never going to get us any closer to freedom. Understanding born of careful analysis is at the very heart of what is distinctive about the Buddhist path. This is the third train-ing, the training in wisdom. Other religions share with Buddhism profound ethics as well as techniques for accessing amazing non-conceptual states. Buddhism claims as its distinction a penetrat-ing, thoughtful analysis of exactly how the world exists. Only by engaging in this analysis, thinking it through and taking it to heart, do we begin to create the basis for real liberation from unneces-sary misery.

Therefore, while it is truly excellent to be a good and kind person and it is vital to learn to focus the mind, this is not enough to get at the root of our misery in cyclic rebirth. Virtue and a quiet mind make us kind and strong, but whether we are moving toward lib-eration depends on how we employ this strength. In order to find freedom, we absolutely must have meditative insight discern-ing—and, eventually, directly perceiving—emptiness, which is the ultimate nature of reality. And in order to have such meditative insight, we must first use reason and analysis to understand and to know the nature of reality. In other words, before we can hope to attain a profound and nondualistic enlightenment, we must first use logical thinking to reach an unshakable mental certainty about the nature of reality.

But how can we develop such certainty? It begins with studying the scriptures and reflecting deeply upon their meaning.

What Texts Should We Study?

Tsong-kha-pa tells us to distinguish between provisional and definitive scriptures. In seeking the correct philosophical view, we first need to study definitive scriptures carefully. We need to understand them well by relying on accurate and authoritative commentaries; we then need to take to heart their message. This understanding then serves as the basis for meditative practice.

What are definitive scriptures? The *Teachings of Akshayamati Sutra* explains that definitive sutras are those that teach empti-ness, the ultimate reality. Emptiness is the end point of the deepest analysis, so sutras that teach it cannot be construed or interpreted as being indicative of some further or hidden meaning beneath the surface. Sutras that teach about conventional truths—such as living beings, compassion, ethics, etc.—are also vitally important on the path to buddhahood, but they are provisional inasmuch as they are not focused on the ultimate, final nature of the things they are discussing. This is because the final nature of all phenomena is emptiness.

From this it should be clear that whether a scripture is definitive or provisional is not based on how literally the text can be read. Sutras that speak in a very clear, unambiguous way about conventional phenomena are provisional because their subject matter is not the final reality. On the other hand, sutras dealing with emptiness are definitive even when certain passages cannot be accepted when taken out of context and read in a hyperliteral manner. For example, sutras that say, "There is no person," should readily be understood, in context, to mean that persons have no ultimate existence—they are empty of essence or self-existence. Persons do exist because they exist in a conventional sense, as convenient designations made in reference to ever-changing collections of mental and physical components. This may initially strike us as a minimal sort of existence, but it is the only kind of existence that anything has. It is the only kind of existence that is possible and, perhaps contrary to our expectations, it is fully robust enough to allow each thing to work, to carry out its respective function.

In definitive sutras such as the Perfection of Wisdom sutras, the Buddha taught that everything is empty—meaning that everything is devoid of any intrinsic existence. Tsong-kha-pa explains that we should understand these teachings by relying on the explanations of Nagarjuna along with those authored by Nagarjuna's spiritual son, Aryadeva.

Nagarjuna's work is the starting point of the Madhyamaka tradition of Buddhist philosophy. Tsong-kha-pa accepts two legitimate ways to divide later Madhyamikas into subschools. First, one can divide them on the basis of whether they accept the existence of external objects, that is, objects that are a different entity from the mind apprehending them. Bhavaviveka is an example of a Madhyamika who accepts external objects. He sharply criticizes Buddhist philosophers who teach that everything is one entity with the mind. The Madhyamaka of Shantarakshita, on the other hand, teaches that there are no external objects even conventionally.

Second, Tsong-kha-pa divides Madhyamikas into two subgroups that are named according to how they use reason to induce understanding of emptiness. Svatantrikas such as Bhavaviveka insist on countering wrong views only with autonomous syllogisms (*svatantra*). These are formal arguments that prove a thesis in a manner that is correct according to the received traditions of Buddhist logic. Prasangikas such as Buddhapalita and Chandrakirti, on the other hand, are comfortable attacking wrong views with consequences (*prasanga*), which are *reductio ad absurdum* arguments. This means that they use arguments that—without necessarily implying any alternative correct position—draw out the internal contradictions of the wrong view they are critiquing.

As we will see in Chapter Eight, Tsong-kha-pa argues in detail that Bhavaviveka's insistence on autonomous syllogisms is not just a difference in logical method but also evidences an underlying difference—a shortcoming—in his view of emptiness. Tsong-kha-pa argues, therefore, that when we set out to understand the Perfection of Wisdom sutras and other definitive sutras, we should rely on the original Madhyamikas—Nagarjuna and Aryadeva—and the commentators in the Prasangika line, such as Buddhapalita, Chandrakirti, and Shantideva.

What Does the Path Eliminate?

We suffer greatly and unnecessarily because we are plagued by ignorant misconceptions of how the world exists. We tend to see ourselves and the things around us as solid, permanent, autonomous, discrete, and substantial, whereas in fact things are evanescent, composite, contingent, and in flux. So the path to freedom is the path of abandoning ignorance by refuting the reified nature, essence, or "self" that ignorance superimposes.

Thus, we can speak of two kinds of "objects of negation." Objects negated by the *path* are ignorances, wrong consciousnesses that we leave behind as we gain wisdom. They are negated in the sense that they are abandoned as we progress on the path. Objects negated by *reason* are the reified natures or essences that wrong consciousnesses superimpose, but that in fact do not exist at all. Reason negates them by refuting them—showing their utter nonexistence—and thus proving that the conception of things as having essential nature is, in fact, a *wrong* consciousness.

Tsong-kha-pa dedicates a significant portion of the *Great Treatise* to clarifying a single question: what exactly *is* the object to be negated by reason? When we use reason to prove that essence or self does not exist, what exactly are we refuting? (We will discuss this further beginning in the next chapter and especially in Chapter Seven.) However, before delving into this, Tsong-kha-pa first discusses the object negated by the path. In this way, he makes it clear that the later exercises in logical reasoning are not merely academic word games but are crucial practices on the path to freedom.

What exactly is it that we must abandon in order to find true happiness and freedom? Following Chandrakirti, Tsong-kha-pa (Volume 3: 206) explains that the remedies the Buddha teaches for hatred, attachment, pride, and so forth are effective against only those specific afflictions. The antidote for ignorance, on the other hand, cures all afflictions.

This shows that ignorance is the basis of all faults and afflictions, the root of all of our problems. In this context, ignorance refers specifically to the mind that wrongly superimposes intrinsic nature. Ignorance is a consciousness that wrongly apprehends people and things as existing by way of their own essential character. Tsong-kha-pa (Volume 3: 206) cites Chandrakirti:

It is said that you become attached to things by the power of an afflictive misunderstanding, a consciousness that superimposes an essence of things, and that one stops cyclic existence by totally stopping that . . . [B]y seeing objects as lacking intrinsic existence, you totally stop the seed of cyclic existence, the consciousness that causes attachment.

Tsong-kha-pa also explains that the particular type of ignorance or wrong consciousness at the root of all misery is called the *view of the perishing aggregates*, a special term that requires some explanation. "Aggregates" refers to the five aggregates of mind and body—form, feeling, discrimination, compositional factors, and consciousness. They are "perishing" because they are all transient, constantly changing, disintegrating moment by moment. There is nothing durable, nothing enduring, among them. The "view of the perishing aggregates" means the view that there is, in relation to these fluctuating elements of my body and mind, an essentially existent person. It is the misconception that I have a personal self that exists intrinsically, by its own built-in power. In other words, it is the misconception that I am a naturally existent person, a person who exists in and of himself, by virtue of his own essential nature.

Buddhist texts often refer to two selflessnesses—the selflessness of persons and the selflessness of phenomena. Selflessness refers to an emptiness—the absence, nonexistence—of an intrinsically existing nature. Here, the word "self" refers to an intrinsically existing nature, an essence, that we unconsciously and erroneously superimpose. We superimpose "self" or intrinsic nature both upon persons and upon other phenomena. The "view of the perishing aggregates" is a specific type of conception of a self or intrinsic nature of persons in that it is the misconception of *oneself* in particular as essentially existent. A mind that refutes this view of the perishing aggregates would therefore be an instance of wisdom realizing the selflessness of persons.

Selflessness of Phenomena

Some Mahayana Buddhist schools teach that the selflessness of persons is a coarse sort of emptiness and that the profound emptiness is the selflessness of phenomena. However, in the Prasangika Madhyamaka school, the two selflessnesses are equally profound. It is only a question of which referent (person/nonperson) one is realizing as empty.

Tsong-kha-pa explains that a realization of the profound emptiness in relation to a person logically entails the capacity to realize, without any difficulty, that same emptiness in relation to any other phenomenon, including the parts of a person's body or mind. He cites Nagarjuna: "If the self does not exist, how could that which belongs to the self exist?" He cites Chandrakirti: "When a chariot is burned, its parts also are burned and thus are not observed; similarly, when meditators know that self does not exist, they will know that what belongs to the self, the things that are the aggregates, also are devoid of self."

This does not mean that when one realizes the selflessness of persons one is, in that very moment, realizing the selflessness of all phenomena. Using an utter nonexistent merely as an analogy, Tsong-kha-pa points out that when you reflect on the nonexistence of the birth-son of a barren woman, you do not in that same moment think, "His ears do not exist." But because you know that the birth-son of a barren woman does not exist, you can immediately realize that his ears do not exist as soon as the question arises. Likewise, Tsong-kha-pa argues, a genuine realization of the selflessness of the person entails the ability to know immediately, upon considering it, the selflessness of other phenomena.

In Buddhism generally, Hinayana or Mahayana, when one meditates on what the person is, one does not find at the basis of the person an "essential self." Rather, meditators engaged in highly focused introspection notice a stream of continuously changing instants of mental experience, and they notice that this stream of experience depends upon the support of the physical body. The person and most other things that we encounter in ordinary experience are composites. They can be broken down into much more basic moments and elements, all of which are constantly changing much more quickly than we can notice. It seems that Hinayana teachings do not explicitly challenge the reality of the basic material elements and point-instants of experience out of which, they say, the person (and everything else) is constructed. Some Hinayana teachings explicitly accept that behind the composites we designate as "the person" or "my body," there are very small, fundamental and irreducible elements. Following Nagarjuna, Tsong-kha-pa teaches that all phenomena—everything that exists, including all particles no matter how small—are empty of essence or inherent reality. Everything that exists must exist interdependently. Thus, there is nothing that has its own being, its own way of existing. Hinayana Buddhist schools teach about what they call the selflessness of persons, but insofar as they cling to the essential reality of irreducible elements or aggregates underlying the person, they have not truly penetrated the profound emptiness at all. They are essentialists who, from the Madhyamaka perspective, have not understood the profound emptiness taught by the Buddha.

3. Our Choices Matter*

What Do We Expect?

IF WE TRY to follow Ha-shang's way, simply pulling our minds back from thoughts entangled with reifying tendencies, we will find that we have gone astray. Our inclinations to reify are too strong and deeply engrained to be eradicated without a direct attack. To stop them, we must first identify them, bring them out into the light, and then use reason to subject them to devastating scrutiny.

Let's consider an analogy. One day I went into a classroom and in order to begin teaching I sat on the table in the front of the room. Suddenly—to the amusement of my students—it collapsed into a pile of debris. I was surprised—I had been sitting on the table for a few hours every week and there was never any problem. Of course, I was certainly never aware of thinking or believing, "There is a permanent table, something I can always rely upon." On the other hand, it really did look very solid. I never noticed it changing—it seemed quite the same every day. Unconsciously, I trusted this appearance deeply. At some level, in an unexamined way, I did expect the table to continue as it was.

Of course this applies to people, as well. When we see a friend often, we do not notice how she is changing. Accepting this without analysis, we implicitly expect that she will continue as she has been. Every day we see her, and she is always living and breathing.

* Based on the *Great Treatise*, Volume 3, Chapters 10 and 11.

Deeply conditioned to this, we find it shocking and somehow wrong when she suddenly dies; it is very hard to accept her death because it clashes with our sense of *how things are*. This is because we still hold a vivid internal image of her—and it is an image of a still-living person.

As Tsong-kha-pa reminds us in the *Great Treatise* (Volume 1: 145–150), the same is true about our own sense of ourselves. Verbally, we acknowledge that we will die, but few of us live in awareness of our own mortality. Until we face life-threatening trauma, death is an abstract idea, not an existential reality. In our unreflective day-to-day experience, the reality of death is occluded, concealed.

Happiness, in Buddhism, depends on seeing reality. We become free only by facing the truth, knowing things as they are. Clinging to mistaken expectations causes us vast and needless misery. In order to know the reality of impermanence and mortality, and to live our lives in the light of that reality, we first must recognize that there is a problem. While we acknowledge impermanence intellectually, we usually act as though we ourselves, along with our friends and possessions, are unchanging.

Therefore, we have to bring to the surface our distorted expectations. We have to recognize that an unconscious expectation that things will continue as they appear now has, in fact, been a powerful influence on our behavior. In meditation, we can then prove to ourselves with devastating clarity that this expectation is wrong because it is discordant with the actual way that things are. We can train our minds to be open to the truths of impermanence and mortality.

Taking Aim

This analogy pertains to impermanence, but it is like this when we set out to realize emptiness. We are addicted to intrinsic nature, the idea that we exist by way of some built-in power to be. Since this habit causes us and those around us vast and needless misery, we have to begin by really seeing that we do have this problem.

We have to identify the misconception that is the target of our analysis.

Through clinging to the illusion of a certain sort of self, we suffer again and again. By believing in *that* kind of self, we are trapped; by seeing that it does not exist, we will become free. Seeking spiritual liberation, we have to locate very precisely just that sense of a "real self" which is the root of our suffering. Tsong-kha-pa writes of this very clearly:

> In order to be sure that a certain person is not present, you must know the absent person. Likewise, in order to be certain of the meaning of "selflessness" or the "lack of intrinsic existence," you must carefully identify the self, or intrinsic nature, that does not exist.

In other words, a crucial first step in the refutation of "self" or "essence" is to accurately identify the target of our arguments. Reason is a powerful tool; if we misidentify the target even slightly, we will probably refute too much or too little.

We can think of the Buddha's teaching, the middle way, as like a path along a narrow ridge from which we may easily fall into extremes of nihilism or eternalism. If we do not carefully limit the object of negation, we will misuse reason to refute too much, falling into nihilism. Ethical commitments to help other living beings break down when logic is misapplied so as to seem to refute the very existence of these beings or to refute any distinction between virtue and nonvirtue. We may come to believe that nothing exists or that our choices, our actions, do not matter.

On the other hand, if we do not refute enough, then the deepest and subtlest forms of ignorance will be untouched by our practice. In consequence, even with all the kindness and mental focus we can muster, we will continue to live in cycles of misery. A precise identification of the deepest root of cyclic existence allows us to find the middle way, a view that slips free from the innate tendency to reify without swerving into nihilism.

Tsong-kha-pa encourages us by pointing out that if we *do* correctly identify the "self" as conceived by the deepest form of ignorance, then refuting that self will naturally entail refuting all mistaken ideas of self. As with a weed, destroying the root destroys the whole plant, but if we miss the deepest root, then the whole thing grows back. When we fully realize that the person lacks even a shred of inherent nature, we will not mistakenly suppose, for example, that the person is immortal due to having a permanent essence. All misconceptions of self are rooted in the deepest misconception. So it is this root misconception, this subtly reified sense of self, that we must identify and attack.

Refuting Too Much

Tsong-kha-pa was particularly concerned that most of the then-prevailing Tibetan interpretations of Nagarjuna's Madhyamaka philosophy misidentified the object of negation. In his view, these widely promulgated misunderstandings of Madhyamaka subvert ethical commitments by treating them—and all other conventions—as provisional in the sense that their validity or legitimacy is obviated by the profound truth of emptiness. Tsong-kha-pa holds that profound emptiness must be understood as complementing and fulfilling, rather than canceling out, the principles of moral action. His writings aim to inspire and—as a matter of historical fact—did inspire vigorous striving in active virtue.

Tsong-kha-pa insists that rational analysis is an indispensable tool in the spiritual life. In order to make cogent the compatibility of emptiness and ethics, Tsong-kha-pa had to show that the two truths, ultimate and conventional, do not contradict, undermine, or supersede one another. Emptiness of essence is the ultimate truth found under exacting analysis of how things exist, but it is fully compatible with valid conventional existence.

In order to explore this view, let's look at what Tsong-kha-pa's *Great Treatise* says about ultimate analysis. All Madhyamaka philosophers agree that there is nothing that exists ultimately. This means that when we use reason to analyze exactly how it is that a person, or a table, or a car exists—just what its final ontological status is—we do not come upon, or find, any definitive basis or ground upon which to establish it. The vivid reality of the car seems to evaporate under analytic scrutiny. The mind seeking to know "what the car *really* is" does not arrive at the ultimate car essence—or at any kind of car at all. If it did, then we would say that a car can withstand ultimate analysis and that a car ultimately exists. Instead, the mind analyzing the car arrives at last at the emptiness of the car—that is, the car's lack of any essential nature. All Madhyamaka philosophers agree that there is nothing that can withstand ultimate analysis. By this they mean that there is nothing anywhere that ultimately exists—including, of course, the Buddha and the teachings of Buddhism. Even emptiness is itself empty; that is, when one searches for the ultimate essence of emptiness, it too is unfindable. One finds only the emptiness of emptiness.

Since not a shred of any object is found under ultimate analysis of how that object exists, some Tibetan interpreters conclude that reason refutes the existence of all things. They argue that when an ultimate mind, a mind tuned in to ultimate reality, turns its eye upon a car and cannot find any trace of the car, this must imply that the car does not exist. Cars may appear to exist to our senses and to our ordinary mental consciousnesses. We may speak of cars in our language. But these are symptoms of delusion, symptoms of ignorance, or—at best—polite fictions. An ultimate mind looking at a car cannot at all find it. This seems to prove its nonexistence.

When Tsong-kha-pa replies that, indeed, cars and tables and people *do* exist, then these others say: Look, either cars are found under Madhyamaka analysis or they are not. If you say that they are, then you are asserting real cars, essentially existent cars, ultimately real cars. You are not a Madhyamika. But if you say that they are not found under analysis, then how can you claim that they exist? Who can say that reasoned analysis refutes the existence of something, but the thing exists anyway?

Tsong-kha-pa argues that ordinary objects exist because they are perceived by unimpaired sense consciousnesses, which are in a very practical way authoritative sources of information. But his opponents meet this with scriptural citations—such as this from the *King of Concentrations Sutra*—suggesting the opposite: "The eye, ear, and nose consciousnesses are not valid cognitions."

Dependent Arising and Emptiness

Tsong-kha-pa devotes a substantial section of the *Great Treatise* to the refutation of viewpoints such as these. But rather than opening with a rebuttal, he begins by showing the heart of his own view, thereby bringing to light the problems in his opponents' position. Tsong-kha-pa cites five different texts where Nagarjuna states clearly that emptiness and dependent arising have the same import, that they are coterminous. They are fully compatible because they are really two ways to talk about the same view of the nature of reality. They are the middle way. For example, Nagarjuna's *Fundamental Treatise* says, "That which arises dependently we explain as emptiness. This [emptiness] is dependent designation; this is the middle way." His *Refutation of Objections* says, "I bow down to the Buddha, the unequaled, supreme teacher, who taught that emptiness, dependent arising, and the middle way hold a single meaning."

For Tsong-kha-pa, the compatibility of emptiness and dependent arising is the very heart of the Madhyamaka view and the key to the path. Dependent arising means that things come into being in dependence upon causes and conditions. Understanding dependent arising correctly refutes the idea that things exist in and of themselves—because they must depend on other things. In the same moment, it also refutes the nihilist extreme—because it shows that things do arise, they do come into existence, and they affect one another. Thus, Tsong-kha-pa advises that if you think that you may have found the profound view of emptiness, you should check to see if you have negated too much. Can this "emptiness" you have discovered be reconciled with the mere existence of things that arise interdependently? If not, then you are certainly mistaken.

Tsong-kha-pa points out that interpretations of Madhyamaka that fail to preserve dependent arising thereby destroy the entire idea of a Buddhist practice. One way to explain this is to discuss the Dharma in terms of the *basis*, the *path*, and *fruit*. The *basis* is everything that exists. Everything that exists is included in one of the two truths: (1) conventional truth and (2) ultimate truth. Ultimate truths are emptinesses; conventional truths are all other things, including living beings. The Mahayana *path* involves two sorts of practice: (1) practices in which one accumulates virtue or merit through one's attitudes toward and relationships with persons (conventional truths); and (2) practices leading to the accumulation of wisdom, certain knowledge of reality (ultimate truth). This path culminates in the *fruit*, perfect buddhahood, which again has two aspects: (1) a buddha's embodiment of form and (2) a buddha's embodiment of truth. The former results from the imprint of the accumulation of merit, the latter results from the imprint of the accumulation of wisdom.

The point is that one cannot become a buddha without both compassionate action and nondual wisdom—and one cannot have these two types of paths without *both* of the two truths, conventional and ultimate. If only emptiness existed and there were, in fact, no conventional truths, then there would be no living beings, no suffering to relieve; thus there would be no compassionate action; and thus there would be no buddhahood. Therefore, maintaining the compatibility of the two truths—the compatibility of emptiness and dependent arising—is crucial to the whole of the Dharma.

Tsong-kha-pa also explains that when we understand the compatibility of dependent arising and emptiness, we see that nihilistic misreadings of Madhyamaka in fact have much in common with the eternalist extremes of those who cling to the idea of intrinsic nature. To understand this, consider that the basic question

—the compatibility of emptiness and dependent arising—can be posed as follows: *Can A produce B when A is empty?* If A is devoid of intrinsic nature, how can it produce B? Suppose that A, the cause, is a seed and B, the effect, is a sprout. Now let's consider three answers to these questions: (1) the answer of the essentialists (including many Buddhists), (2) the answer of those who, in interpreting Madhyamaka, negate too much, and (3) the answer of Tsong-kha-pa.

Essentialists: A seed cannot produce a sprout if the seed is empty of intrinsic nature. If the seed does not have, in its intrinsic nature, the capacity to produce a sprout, then a sprout will not be produced from the seed. Since sprouts are produced, we know that their causes, seeds, must have in their essential nature the power to produce sprouts.

Those who negate too much: We agree that a seed cannot produce a sprout when the seed is empty of intrinsic nature. If the seed does not have, in its intrinsic nature, the capacity to produce a sprout, then a sprout will not be produced from the seed. However, Madhyamaka analysis shows that seeds have no intrinsic nature; thus, it follows that sprouts are not produced. All production, all existence, is a delusion.

Tsong-kha-pa: A seed can produce a sprout when the seed is empty of intrinsic nature, as is frequently observed in the world. A seed does not need an intrinsic nature in order to produce a sprout. In fact, it is only because seeds lack intrinsic nature that dependent arising can take place as observed.

By framing the discussion in these terms, Tsong-kha-pa makes it clear that the Tibetans who negate too much, while priding themselves on their rigorous Madhyamaka analysis, in fact share a common assumption with the essentialists: Production must be intrinsic production; existence must be intrinsic existence. Once one accepts this assumption, one falls either to the extreme of reification—by affirming intrinsic nature—or to the extreme of nihilism—by denying production. Neither party can imagine that things might *merely* exist and *merely* give rise to effects without doing so by virtue of some essential property or intrinsic nature. Yet Tsong-kha-pa is able to cite a large number of passages from Nagarjuna and Chandrakirti showing that this is precisely the position they take: Things arise and give rise to other things without a shred of intrinsic nature.

In seeking to understand emptiness, it is vital not to damage our confidence in dependent arising. Tsong-kha-pa teaches that dependent arising itself is the best reasoning we can use to demonstrate that things are empty of intrinsic nature. We can practice this every day. When we see some impressive object—a mountain or a large, new building—we can immediately reflect on how this object arises from causes and conditions. For example, a large school building depends upon earlier people having certain ideas about education. It depends upon a society in which shared values support the work that is done in the building. It depends on money raised from many people, and thus upon their work, their economic system. It depends upon people dreaming of this particular school, architects and engineers designing it, people creating and assembling materials, people making the walls one block at a time. The wood in the building depends on trees, which depend on water, earth, and light. Without hard work to maintain the building, it quickly disintegrates.

The school does not have any natural capacity to exist on its own. That is to say, it is empty of any natural power to be there. It would not be there without its causes and it will vanish as the conditions supporting it change. Notice that the building, on first impression, does *not* appear so contingent. It does not show us how it really is. It presents itself as imposing, as though suggesting that it had some natural power to be there. In subtle ways, this is true with all the objects we see.

Deeper Understanding

In this way, it is not hard to get started on thinking about how dependent arising and emptiness are compatible. However, full development of this understanding is difficult. We must maintain certainty about cause and effect relationships—that all of the different causes and conditions produce their own distinct effects—while at the same time developing complete certainty that all of these conditions and all of their effects are completely devoid of any shred of intrinsic nature. Echoing Nagarjuna, Tsong-kha-pa warns that complete certainty about both dependent arising and emptiness is very rare. Tsong-kha-pa advises that to find this right view, we must keep our ethical commitments and cultivate both merit and wisdom. We need to study hard with good teachers and we need to reflect on their teachings, taking them to heart.

As an example of how one might go astray, Tsong-kha-pa describes the thinking of practitioners who have misunderstood the teachings on emptiness. They set out to do Madhyamaka analysis and they soon notice that when they search for a table, or a pot, or a person, or a school, the thing they are searching for cannot be identified with any of its parts. Concluding that there is no object, they then reflect that the same analysis would refute the very existence of their own analyzing mind. Wondering how it is that they could be doing the analysis that shows that the analyzing mind itself does not exist, they are faced with a paradox. They throw up their hands and conclude, "Things are neither existent nor nonexistent."

This kind of approach is marked by careless and shallow reasoning. It will not lead to certainty about emptiness, nor to the powerful understanding of how it is that only empty phenomena can act as causes and effects. It is true that Nagarjuna and other Madhyamaka teachers give arguments that show how, when one analyzes carefully, one cannot find or pin down the target of analysis. Those who negate too much conclude that these arguments refute the very existence of the things being analyzed. But as Tsong-kha-pa shows, Nagarjuna's arguments in fact refute the existence of things in a manner that would allow them to be found under this kind of searching analysis. In other words, Nagarjuna shows that things do not exist *ultimately*. His arguments prove that things do not exist *essentially*. Things have not even the slightest element of any findable-under-ultimate-analysis kind of existence. Even though Nagarjuna often does not add qualifying words like "ultimately," sometimes he does. And he certainly cannot mean to prove the utter nonexistence of ordinary things. For if he did, then why would Nagarjuna talk about this reasoning as part of a path from misery to liberation? Suffering, people, path, and liberation—they all would be nonexistent.

To explain this idea—that it is just empty things that exist and are active in cause and effect relations—Tsong-kha-pa cites Chandrakirti:

> Empty things, such as reflections, depend on a collection
>   of causes—
> It is not as though this were not well known.
> From those empty reflections and so forth
> Arise consciousnesses that bear their image.
> Similarly, even though all things are empty,
> From those empty things effects are definitely produced.

The passage makes an analogy between a reflection—which is empty of actually being the object that it appears to be—and ordinary things like tables and people, which falsely appear to exist in and of themselves, but do not. Reflections, although completely devoid of being what they appear to be, nonetheless arise from causes and conditions and are able to act so as to bring about effects, such as someone becoming aware of the reflected image.

Analogously, tables and people appear to exist in and of

themselves, but in fact they are completely empty of any such nature. Yet this in no way prevents them from relying on causes and acting as causes of other effects. What we do matters because we exist and our actions, our choices, are the conditions from which the future arises.

4. Ultimate and Conventional Radio*

Ultimate Analysis

THE BUDDHA INVITED his followers to analyze their own conceptions of person and self. He taught that however one analyzes the mind and body of a person, the essential personal self that we believe in is nowhere to be found. The person is empty of intrinsic nature. Yet the Buddha uses words like "I" and "mine" to refer to himself, his own motivations, and his own experiences. Moreover, the notion of personal identity is critical to Buddhist ethics, in which karma is created and bears fruit as moral consequences in this life and future lives. This is one form of dependent arising. As we have seen, Tsong-kha-pa's central point in rebutting nihilistic misreadings of Madhyamaka is to show that the heart of the Madhyamaka view is the compatibility of dependent arising and emptiness. Interpretations of emptiness that do not protect dependent arising cannot be correct.

How, then, can Tsong-kha-pa answer the arguments of these other scholars? They argue that if chariots and persons cannot withstand Madhyamaka analysis, if their reality recedes when we search for them with careful reasoning, then this means that reason refutes them. How can anyone talk about things that reason has refuted as having any kind of meaningful existence at all?

Tsong-kha-pa argues that this question comes about through

* Based on the *Great Treatise*, Volume 3, Chapters 12 and 14.

conflating (1) the inability to withstand rational analysis with (2) invalidation or refutation by reason. Indeed, a careful thinker will not claim that things are *refuted by reason* and yet exist nonetheless. But things may exist and do exist very well while being *unable to withstand rational analysis*. What is the difference?

To ask whether something can withstand rational analysis is to ask whether it is "found" or demonstrated by a line of reasoning that analyzes deeply, intent on digging down to the core reality behind an appearance. When such reasoning analyzes a car, it does not find any such essential reality. None of the parts, individually, is the car. The whole collection of car parts cannot be the car, for the collection of parts could be strewn around or heaped up randomly. The shape of the car is not the car, for we can have this shape in a model without having a car. Is there some other thing we can pin down, apart from its parts, the collection of the parts, and the shape of the assembled collection, that is the very essence of the car? What can we point at? That one finds no car-essence that can serve as the basis of the car is what it means to say that a car is "unable to withstand rational analysis."

However, that ultimate analysis does not find a car does not entail that it refutes the car. Rather, it refutes an essentially existent car, *the kind of car that it would have found had such a car been there to find*. Cars, chariots, and persons exist, but this existence is established by ordinary conventional consciousnesses that give us practical and accurate information about the world around us. We should not expect them to be found under ultimate analysis in search for an essence, and we should not suppose that their not being found in this way undermines their mere existence.

Tsong-kha-pa gives a simple analogy that has helped me immensely: *We do not see sounds no matter how carefully we look, but this does not refute them.* Ultimate analysis and conventional consciousnesses are here compared to two different sense powers. Each gives correct information about its domain. Likewise, when we are not satisfied with a car as we know it now, or as a mechanic or engineer might explain it, but press on to search out its ultimate ontological basis, the unfindability of such an ultimate essence has no bearing on the ordinary sense of the question, "Is this a good car?" Cars exist and run without any essence, without any findable car-nature.

In other words, the unfindability of the car under ultimate analysis is not a sign of the car's nonexistence. Rather, it is a sign that the car does not exist in such a manner as to make it findable under just this sort of analysis. That is, unfindability under analysis is a sign of the nonexistence of an essentially existent car.

Following Chandrakirti's reading of Nagarjuna, Tsong-kha-pa argues that if things had any sort of essence or intrinsic nature of their own, this essential nature would have to be located under ultimate analysis. Therefore, the fact that things are not found under ultimate analysis means that they lack intrinsic nature. The lack of intrinsic nature is logically equivalent and universally coterminous with the lack of ultimate existence. For Chandrakirti and Tsong-kha-pa, not existing under ultimate analysis, not existing ultimately, and not existing intrinsically or essentially are three ways of saying the same thing. However, again: This is *not* the same as saying these things do not exist at all.

Thinking about Tsong-kha-pa's analogy—we never see sounds, but this does not refute them—I concocted for my students the analogy of two radio stations. Channel A is "all things considered radio." This is our regular, *conventional* channel, and on it we get all kinds of information about the diversity and complexity of the world. Perhaps today they are airing a fierce debate: the proponents of red cars are angry, in a raging controversy with the proponents of blue cars. Normally we listen *only* to this station, so we take it all at face value and without deeper scrutiny. We are unaware that there is or could be any other channel. But in fact there is a second station, broadcast on channel B, the *ultimate* perspective. Channel B's programming is "all emptiness, all the time radio." Every phenomenon is presented only from the point of view of its ultimate nature. But when we tune into this channel, all of the detailed information from the other channel is unavailable.

From the perspective of ultimate reality, red cars and blue cars are equally and exclusively empty.

Channel B, emptiness radio, adds new information and a deeper perspective on what is being discussed on the conventional channel. It shows that the things discussed on channel A definitely do not exist in the way that they are ordinarily presented. When we come back to channel A after tuning in to B, we now understand just how it is that channel A is merely conventional; it is not the only or final perspective. But this new information does not, of course, prove that red cars are in all ways identical to blue cars. We still have to make distinctions and make choices about what, if anything, to drive. Channel B alone does not allow us to make practical distinctions, so we still need the information from channel A.

Thus, ultimate analysis does not find the car, but it also definitely does not find or indicate the car to be nonexistent. If it did, then since ultimate analysis is a valid source of knowledge, the car would have to be nonexistent. Ultimate analysis simply does not find the kind of car reality that would be findable under that kind of analysis. This is a very important distinction, and making this distinction clearly is one of Tsong-kha-pa's major contributions to the history of Tibetan philosophy. Conventional realities are not wiped out by their profound emptiness of essence; instead, they have their own kind of validity, as objects known by conventional consciousnesses. The problem of knowing which car to drive is the general problem of how to choose between possible courses of action. It is the question of how empty persons can make distinctions between right and wrong. Tsong-kha-pa shows that answering this question requires distinguishing between two types of knowledge about persons, as well as cars and other things.

Some Tibetan interpreters of the Madhyamaka suggest that speaking of the existence of cars and persons is, in effect, a concession to the moral situation and limited understanding of those who are not philosophically sophisticated. On this reading, the Madhyamaka acceptance of conventional existence amounts to no more than an admission that other people, folks like shepherds and mechanics, will insist upon talking about sheep and cars as if they actually existed. We, the philosophers and spiritual practitioners, are beyond such conventions and for our own part know perfectly well that rational analysis refutes the existence of such things.

Tsong-kha-pa sharply rejects this interpretation of conventional existence. He stresses that the ordinary conventional consciousnesses that provide accurate information about practical distinctions can be found and are required just as much among philosophers and advanced meditators as they are among shepherds and mechanics. It is such consciousnesses that establish the standard of conventional validity. As it happens, most philosophers may know little about the relative merits of different cars, but some automotive philosophers might know a great deal and the rest are equipped to learn about this if they choose. Philosophers know that the distinction between a good car and a bad car cannot withstand ultimate analysis, but when it matters to them, they are fully equipped to learn to make the distinction anyway.

In the *Great Treatise*, ultimate analysis is enlightening and liberating. Yet complete spiritual fulfillment also requires the ability to act compassionately, and that involves making practical distinctions. Therefore, Tsong-kha-pa insists upon the clarifying power of analysis that is not ultimate, analysis that operates within the constraints and boundaries of conventional fact and language so as to illuminate what does and what does not exist, what is and what is not helpful. Not all useful analysis need immediately reduce everything to emptiness. In other words, we can learn valuable, practical things by analyzing which car is good to drive, which action is good to do, which seed is good to plant, without at each step interrogating the final ontological status of the car, action, or seed.

Realists or essentialists—believing that things exist as they appear, on their own power—might feel validated upon hearing Tsong-kha-pa's argument that Madhyamaka analysis does not refute the existence of cars and tables. They may say, "It is just as we told you. Cars are real because, just as you have explained, they are in no way refuted by deconstructive analysis. We can proceed just as we did before." However, Tsong-kha-pa is not at all rescuing the realists and essentialists. If things did exist in the way that they ordinarily appear to us, they would have to be found under ultimate analysis. Things appear as though naturally set up, self-instituting; yet when we search, we cannot find a shred of essence that would allow this.

Therefore, while remembering that ultimate analysis does not refute the arising of one thing in dependence upon another, we must not think that ultimate analysis is on that account trivial, like some sort of philosophical trick or game. "Intrinsic nature" is not like a hat that we put on (when we first hear about it) and then take off (when we hear it refuted), leaving the world as we see it now unscathed.[2] A pervasive sense that things are real and solid and exist just as they appear is woven right into the fabric of the world as we experience it. While tables do exist, we have yet to see them just as they are. Our very perception of them—while a valid source of information—is at the same time contaminated with a layer of distortion. That distortion is the appearance of the table as something that is able to be there on its own power, something that exists in and of itself.

Thus when we begin to see, or even to suspect, that things lack essence and are not at all as we had supposed, we may feel terrified, as though our world is coming apart at the seams or evaporating beneath our feet. We calm those fears by again remembering that it is *not* that there is nothing. There is dependent arising, just as there has always been. Analysis threatens nothing but the false overlay, the distorting superimposition, which has caused us and others so much misery.

Conventional Existence

Tsong-kha-pa thus explains that Madhyamaka refutes intrinsic existence, but follows worldly convention in accepting the mere existence of tables and chairs and people. This raises the question: Does it not seem that what we think of as "worldly convention" enshrines some things that are actually wrong? What about the notion of a divine creator who oversees the affairs of the world and the dispensation of justice?

In refuting such views, Buddhist philosophers use rational analyses and arguments. From this, according to Tsong-kha-pa, many Tibetan philosophers concluded that persons and tables have the same status as the divine creator because both are refuted by analysis and yet sustained in the conventional beliefs of many ordinary people. Such Tibetan philosophers cannot accept even the conventional existence of a person or car, for they think that to do so would also entail accepting all the other conventions known in the world, including the convention of a creator God. They believe that to deny the conventional existence of constructs such as a divine creator commits them also to denying the conventional existence of chariots and persons. As a result, they have no way to make any conventional distinctions on their own behalf; they hold that all distinctions are made by ignorance and are sometimes compassionately tolerated by the philosopher as a concession to the ignorant. For their own part, they claim neither to identify nor to assert any phenomenon. In the context of such an understanding, meditating on emptiness means to stabilize the mind without apprehending anything at all.

Tsong-kha-pa strongly and repeatedly disagrees with this sort of approach, which he regards as a grievous and nihilistic deviation from the Buddhist philosophical middle way. He argues that Madhyamaka philosophers have to be able to make conventional distinctions and to explain how the world works at the conventional level, while using reason to refute even the conventional existence of constructs such as a creator God.

Tsong-kha-pa's *Great Treatise* lays out three criteria for saying that something exists conventionally: (1) a conventional consciousness knows about it; (2) no other conventional valid cognition contradicts its being as it is thus known; and (3) reason that accurately analyzes its final reality—that is, analyzes whether something intrinsically exists—does not contradict it. Since nothing exists ultimately, whatever fails to meet these criteria for existing conventionally does not exist at all.

The first criterion of conventional existence is that conventional consciousness must know about it. Tsong-kha-pa tells us that, in a sense, all conventional consciousnesses operate in a noninquisitive manner; to some degree they function within the context of how something appears to them, without asking, "Is this how the object *really* exists, or does it just appear this way to the mind?" At the same time, and vitally, he points out that conventional consciousnesses need not be *utterly* noninquisitive. They operate within the context of how things appear, but *within that context they can do analysis.* In other words, they can analyze questions like, "Is this car a good one to drive?" "Is this action a good one to do?" This analysis can be quite deep, as long as it stops short of questioning the mode of being, or ontological status. In other words, it does not ask the question, "What is a car, *really*?"

Everyone has this kind of ordinary analytical consciousness. We may sometimes ask philosophical questions like, "Is conventional knowledge *really* accurate?" or "Does this object exist this way in reality?" Nevertheless, we cannot think this way all the time. We have to make mundane distinctions about the time of day, what is and is not edible, the weather, and so forth. We also have to make other analytical distinctions that are highly specialized to our professions. So, Tsong-kha-pa reminds us that conventional knowledge is not only what is accepted by the nonphilosophical village elders, etc. Conventional knowledge is something that advanced practitioners and sophisticated philosophers also must have and rely upon. Conventional knowledge is evident on every side of every philosophical argument. It shows up, for instance, in the examples that we use to make arguments with one another. It is the perceptual and experiential basis for all of our languages.

However, as Tsong-kha-pa's latter two criteria for conventional existence make clear, some things that conventional consciousness seems to know about are in fact nonexistent. That is, careful analysis and accurate perception even at the conventional level can show that what some persons or consciousnesses take for fact is actually completely wrong. For example, an ordinary conventional consciousness might mistake a rope for a snake or a mirage for water. One does not have to analyze emptiness in order to refute these mistaken conceptions and perceptions. Belief in a flat earth, and other hypotheses refuted by science, all fall into this same category.

There are other things that seem to be a matter of ordinary, conventional experience—and which accurate conventional knowledge does *not* contradict—but which are nonetheless wrong. As Tsong-kha-pa puts it, "There are things that have been apparently 'known to the world' from beginningless time, and yet do not exist even conventionally inasmuch as reason contradicts them." As examples, one can cite the misconception (and misperception) that things have essential nature, or the idea that yesterday's mountain is the same as today's mountain. Only analysis of how things really exist allows these ideas to be refuted. Yet they are refuted, and thus they do not exist even conventionally. Thus, it is not the case that Madhyamikas accept everything that ordinarily seems to be common knowledge in the world.

On the other hand, Tsong-kha-pa accepts the conventional validity of cars and tables and people that appear as objects of ordinary, healthy consciousnesses, minds that have not been fooled or distorted by factors such as disease, optical illusion, bad philosophy, and so forth. He argues, as we have seen, that all reasoned analysis can and must proceed from this basic set of accurate and reliable data. Even though the senses mistakenly present images of cars and tables that appear as though they were objectively, independently, and essentially real, they do allow us to accurately distinguish between a car and a table. With further analysis at the conventional level, we can even learn which tables to sit on (if any) and which cars (if any) are good to drive.

5. Reliable Sources*

Our Senses as a Source of Knowledge

WHEN TSONG-KHA-PA advises us to read the scriptures and classical treatises, to study hard and to think about what we have read, he is advising us to do as he did. His close reading of Madhyamaka texts, his own fine analysis, led him to understanding their meaning with a particular and powerful clarity. The *Great Treatise* is personal spiritual advice from Tsong-kha-pa, but this—of course—does not mean something separate from helping us get at the meaning of Buddhist scriptures. Tsong-kha-pa shows us how he reads Nagarjuna and how he reads Chandrakirti so as to avoid the mistakes that many earlier interpreters had made. In other words, the *Great Treatise* is both personal guidance and scholarly commentary. Tsong-kha-pa aims to assist us in clearing away doubts as we seek to establish the meaning of the Dharma teaching in our minds.

A case in point is the issue of the validity of the information we get from conventional consciousnesses. As we noted in Chapter Three, Tsong-kha-pa argues that we know ordinary objects exist because they are perceived by unimpaired sense consciousnesses, states of mind that are authoritative sources of practical information. But his opponents meet this with scriptural citations—such as this from the *King of Concentrations Sutra*—suggesting the opposite: "The eye, ear, and nose consciousnesses are not valid

* Based on the *Great Treatise*, Volume 3, Chapters 13, 15 and 24.

cognitions." Likewise, Chandrakirti says, "The world is not valid in any way."

Tsong-kha-pa makes a careful reading of Chandrakirti's own explanation of this issue, showing that these passages clearly mean that ordinary worldly consciousnesses are not valid sources of information "in the context of reality" or "with regard to reality." The terms translated as "reality" here are just-that-ness (*de kho na nyid*) and suchness (*de bzhin nyid*). These terms refer to the ultimate reality, the final nature of things. They refer to emptiness. Accordingly, Tsong-kha-pa explains that Chandrakirti clearly means to teach that we cannot rely on our ordinary sense faculties to tell us whether something is or is not empty of intrinsic nature. When we look at the table, even our eyes present an image of something that seems to be set up right there, as though apart from us and independent of its causes and parts. In this regard, a visual consciousness is "not valid in any way." In this regard, it is "not a valid cognition." If we want accurate information about whether things exist naturally, in and of themselves, we must tune in to "channel B" by analyzing, using reason, interrogating the ontology of the table. As Chandrakirti points out, if our ordinary senses already gave us an accurate picture of ultimate reality, what would be the point of working to develop an enlightened mind?

Tsong-kha-pa explains, painstakingly, that our ordinary conventional consciousnesses—when not impaired by optical illusions, drugs, bad philosophy, and so forth—are reliable sources of information about what exists and what does not exist. They are, in that sense, "valid" or authoritative. They can tell us whether there is or is not a table in this room. They can tell us whether the moon is shining. They can tell us where the road is turning. We can rely on them for this sort of knowledge.

In some other schools of Buddhist philosophy, valid cognition is said to be valid because it knows accurately the "nature" of its object. These schools also claim that objects exist by way of their natures. Consequently, their sense of valid cognition implies getting at the essential nature of an object and certifying that the object really does exist on account of that essential nature being seen there. Chandrakirti attacks any idea of this kind of valid cognition, in which validity is possible only on the basis of a real essence. Taking these passages out of context, some might think that Chandrakirti was giving a general refutation of the validity of conventional knowledge. And yet this would contradict Chandrakirti's clear statement: "The world knows objects with four valid cognitions."

Chandrakirti's own view, as Tsong-kha-pa explains it, is that there *is* valid conventional knowledge, but it is not knowledge of objects that exist by way of their own nature. Rather, conventional minds get at objects that are, in one important sense, false. A table is not an ultimate reality. It does exist, but it does not exist as it appears. When we search analytically, looking for this apparently independent table, we cannot find it. Thus a table exists, but it is at the same time "false" inasmuch as it does not exist in the manner in which it appears. It is these conventional, falsely appearing objects—objects that *do exist*—that are the objects of conventional knowledge. As discussed above, reliable knowledge of conventional objects, appearing falsely to our senses, is indispensable to the path. We find final freedom and fulfillment in buddhahood through wisdom only when it is in synergy with compassion and virtuous action. The mind of compassion must apprehend suffering beings, and these beings will of course appear—falsely— as though they were objectively and independently real. As we deepen our understanding of emptiness, we grow increasingly to distrust and to disbelieve this false appearance, but the false appearance remains until we are buddhas.

This is a strange truth, and it is the crux of the matter: we have from our senses reliable information about the ordinary things in the world even though our senses are at the same time deceived about just how these things really exist. In trying to make this clear, Tsong-kha-pa and his followers will say, for example, that our eyes and ears are "mistaken" (*'khrul ba*) but not "wrong" (*log pa*). They are mistaken because they are constantly presenting images of their objects as existing substantially, naturally, independently. They are reliable and not wrong because the colors, shapes, sounds, tastes, smells, and textures they disclose do exist.

You might think that since conventional consciousnesses are reliable sources of knowledge and since they perceive things as existing naturally, it must follow that things *do* exist naturally in a conventional sense. On this view, there is no intrinsic nature ultimately, but conventionally we distinguish tables from chairs and red cars from blue cars by way of their having different intrinsic characters. Tsong-kha-pa argues that this is the view of Bhavaviveka, who is classified as a Svatantrika Madhyamika, and—following Chandrakirti—he rejects this view. Understanding this well is not an easy matter. As Tsong-kha-pa says, "Since we refute essential or intrinsic existence *even conventionally* . . . it seems to be very difficult to posit conventional objects." Perhaps thinking of many of his Tibetan contemporaries, he adds, "This causes most individuals to fall into an overly negative view."

Tables and cars and persons exist conventionally. For Tsong-kha-pa, saying that something exists conventionally means that it does exist because it is found by a reliable mind, such as an unimpaired visual consciousness recognizing a shape. Tables, etc. are not findable under ultimate analysis, so they do not exist ultimately, but as we have seen, they are not at all refuted by analysis. On the other hand, the notion of intrinsic nature or essential character is refuted by analysis. Essential nature does not exist at all. Hence it does not exist even conventionally.

This is too much for most of us to comprehend all at once as we set out to study. There is one key thing always to remember in trying to sort this out. The balancing point—the middle way—is dependent arising. One thing arises in dependence upon another. Our choices affect what happens next. Each thing arises precisely in a given moment not because of its own unique essence, but because of relations among a vast network of conditions—in which every node is equally devoid of essential or intrinsic nature.

How Things Arise

One of the arguments Nagarjuna uses to refute essential existence is to show that things do not arise from themselves, they do not arise from other things, they do not arise from both themselves and other things, and they do not arise causelessly. Nagarjuna and Chandrakirti make it clear that these four types of production are each refuted even conventionally. In this case, how can Tsong-kha-pa help us read these Madhyamaka authors as still allowing and protecting dependent arising?

Tsong-kha-pa explains that Nagarjuna and Chandrakirti are refuting the notion of production that is findable under analysis. People who believe in "real production" or "real existence" think that these things have some kind of locatable essence. When we lay out all the possibilities and sort through them, we ought to be able to pin down just how it is that the production is taking place. However, as we analyze each possibility carefully, we fail to find—for example—any way that we can pin down and describe the exact mechanics of how one thing arises from some other, completely different thing. The same is true of the other three possibilities.

Things that exist only conventionally arise in dependence upon things that exist only conventionally, and they do so in a manner that is both reliable and mysterious. It is reliable because we can count on certain kinds of conditions giving rise to certain kinds of effects: lighting a fire will not cool things off; a pear seed will not grow into an apple tree. We can analyze and explain, in conventional and scientific terms, why these things are so.

But it is also deeply mysterious because, in our efforts to analyze and categorize, we can never get to the very bottom of how dependent arising works. Suppose, for example, we think that production *is* truly real—can be taken as existing as it appears—because things are produced from *other* things. We may suppose that a cause is one thing and its effect is something of a different nature, something apart from the cause in space and later than the cause in time. But can a cause actually bring about an effect without ever contacting it in time or space? If they never touch at all, then how does one give rise to the other? Through some intervening medium? And then, wouldn't one say that the intervening medium acts as the actual immediate cause? Suppose, then, that the actual immediate cause, whatever it may be, *does* contact the effect. Does that mean that the cause and the effect become, at some point, simultaneously existent in precisely the same place? If not, how can one say that they have made contact? Must there not still be some intervening medium? On the other hand, suppose that the cause and effect do make contact by being simultaneously present in the same place. Can you then have a cause that does not precede the effect? And if in fact they must be at exactly the same place and the same time in order for one to affect the other, then in what sense are they really *other*?

Tsong-kha-pa argues that this sort of analysis refutes essentially real production. That is, it refutes any notion of a kind of production that can be found under analysis. It does not refute mere production; *it does not refute dependent arising.* Tsong-kha-pa cites Chandrakirti to make it very clear that he is not just concocting this:

> Because things are not produced
> Causelessly, or from causes such as a divine creator,
> Or from themselves, or from both self and other,
> They are produced dependently.

Chandrakirti states that dependent production is what is proven by the elimination of the four possibilities. This makes it very clear that for Chandrakirti mere production, the flow of dependent arising, is *not* itself one of these four.

It is not that we need more possibilities to consider; it is that we have an alternative to fixing upon any of them. The four fully cover any possible type of analytically locatable production, production as it appears to our minds. Because none of these four types of production can be found, we know that the way that production appears to our minds is not the way it actually is. Things do, of course, arise. Dependent arising means that "this arises from that" in a manner that is not able to bear ultimate analytical scrutiny—but which works anyway.

Tsong-kha-pa cites a passage from Chandrakirti in which an opponent points out that it is contradictory to say that dependently produced things are "not produced" in the four ways. After all, if they are dependently produced, then they *are* produced. Chandrakirti responds by spelling it out very clearly, "We contend that dependently produced things are, like reflections, not produced *intrinsically*." In other words, the refutation of the four types of production refutes any kind of production that would have its own intrinsic nature and would thus be findable under analysis. It refutes intrinsically existent production. But it does not mean that things are not produced. They are produced inasmuch as they are dependent arisings.

In this passage Chandrakirti himself adds in the word "intrinsically" to make himself very clear, but in a great many passages Nagarjuna and Chandrakirti omit this kind of clarifying qualification. Tsong-kha-pa, on the other hand, is careful about adding qualifiers and extends himself in arguing for their importance. He cites Mahayana sutras to prove that the Buddha himself states that these qualifiers are implicit even where they are not spelled out. For example, in the *Descent into Lanka Sutra* the Buddha says, "Mahamati, thinking that they are not produced intrinsically, I said that all phenomena are not produced."

Skillful Teaching

Tsong-kha-pa was very concerned about refuting nihilist misreadings of Madhyamaka that had become prevalent in Tibet. On the other hand, the original Madhyamaka writers were much more concerned about refuting the realist and essentialist philosophies of their Buddhist and non-Buddhist contemporaries. These realists took it for granted that "production" or "existence" must refer to something that has some analytically locatable nature. When Nagarjuna refutes "production," he is refuting the kind of production many of his readers—fellow philosophers—advocated. To them it would be redundant to use expressions such as "production of things with intrinsic nature" or "truly existent production."

To a great extent, the realist philosophies of Nagarjuna's audience correspond to our innate tendencies to reify, to exaggerate the kind of existence things have. For that reason, Nagarjuna's style of writing has great power for us today. It cuts hard against our deep tendency to accept the false appearance that the things we see have their own objective natures.

On the other hand, our world today has its full share of nihilistic philosophies. Many of us—like many of Tsong-kha-pa's contemporaries—need to be reminded of how, in the face of utter emptiness, it is possible, reasonable, and necessary to make moral choices. "In dependence on this, that arises," means that while nothing exists in and of itself, our choices matter enormously because they give shape to the future of the world.

6. Ultimate Reality Exists Conventionally*

Absences Exist and Can Be Important

As WE HAVE SEEN, emptiness—the ultimate reality—is the absence or lack of intrinsic nature. This *lack* exists. Emptiness exists. We usually think of existence in relation to what is actually present; for example, we say, "There is a chair in this room." But absences also exist and are sometimes very important. In my classes, I point out to my students that a lack of elephant exists in the room. Without this absence, there would be at least one elephant present. This likely would interfere with our teaching and learning plans for the day. Hence, the lack of elephant is an existing condition that is quite important for class to proceed undisturbed.

Yet it would seem that there are an infinite number of such absences everywhere—there is the absence of the planet Mars in the Potomac River, and so forth. In each place, there exists the absence of each and every thing except those few that are there. Thus, these infinite absences—while necessary for the world to function—are in another sense trivial. We could start making a catalog of them, and we would never reach the end, nor is it obvious that we become any wiser or kinder in the process of cataloging. When would they ever matter?

To take the elephant example, suppose that a student begins to suffer from a delusion that there *is* an elephant in the classroom.

* Based on the *Great Treatise*, Volume 3, Chapters 15 and 16.

His emotional and behavioral reactions to this imagined ele-phant—whether fear or curiosity or perhaps greed (elephants are valuable)—will be unhelpful to him and unhelpful to the rest of the class. Suddenly, the existence of one particular absence, absence of elephant in the classroom, becomes extremely important. We have to get serious about the question of how to help him by proving the absence of elephant, an absence that is obvious to the rest of us but not to him.

In some ways it is like this with the intrinsic nature that seems to imbue things with objective reality. Such intrinsic nature does not exist at all. It is absent everywhere, but this in itself does not explain why it is important. Rabbit horns and frog manes are also absent everywhere. These considerations only arise when some-one actually believes in one of these things and has some trou-ble on that account. In the case of intrinsic nature, Tsong-kha-pa's view is that we are habituated through beginningless rebirth to the delusion that things have this nonexistent quality. It is a profound addiction. And on the basis of this addictive delusion, we suffer immeasurable torment. For that reason, emptiness—absence of intrinsic nature—is the most important thing we could ever under-stand. The existence of this particular absence is monumentally important to us all.

Ultimate Reality Exists Conventionally

There is yet another way in which the emptiness that is the mere absence of intrinsic nature is different from—and more important than—the emptiness that is the mere absence of an elephant in the room. Emptiness of intrinsic nature is the ultimate reality. Empti-ness of intrinsic nature is the ultimate nature of the table. Empti-ness is the ultimate nature of the cup. Emptiness is not just another absence, like the absence of Mars in my classroom. It is the ulti-mate nature of each and every thing that exists. This is because when an analytical mind asks, "What is this table, really?" and searches deeply, it fails to find any core or essence of being in the table. The mind that sees or knows this lack of essence is called an "ultimate mind," a mind that gets at the basis of things. The lack of intrinsic nature that is known by such a mind is the profound emptiness, the ultimate truth.

Because it is the final nature of every existent, emptiness that is the sheer absence of intrinsic nature is the ultimate reality. While this reality is very important—because we all suffer immeasurably through clinging to intrinsic nature—it is not something rare that we have to look for far away. This ultimate reality is always immediately present as the final nature of every thing in every moment. What *is* very rare and very precious is the wisdom consciousness that understands this reality.[3]

Since emptiness exists and is the ultimate truth, you might suppose that emptiness itself exists in an ultimate sense. But this is incorrect. Everything that exists, exists only conventionally. Everything that exists is included in the two truths, ultimate truth (emptiness) and conventional truth (everything else). But both of these truths exist only conventionally. To exist ultimately, something would have to "bear analysis" by an ultimate mind searching for the final basis of its being. When the mind of ultimate analysis looks at a cup, it finds only the emptiness of the cup. When it looks at this emptiness, it does *not* find some essentially real thing called emptiness as the basis of all. Emptiness, like all other existents, lacks intrinsic nature.

This is a profound point in Madhyamaka Buddhism. It is not that everything else is unreal as compared to the one real thing, which is real in and of itself. There are other philosophies that teach this. But in Madhyamaka there is only one level of existence or type of existence: conventional existence. One particular conventionally existing phenomenon—emptiness—is the utter absence of any other level or type of existence. Among all the things that exist conventionally, things' lack of existing on their own, in and of themselves, is called the ultimate truth because it is the truth realized by a mind that analyzes how things ultimately exist.

On Having No View

When a mind of ultimate analysis finds that there is no "essence" in things, this lack of essence is not thereby confirmed as a new type of essence. Therefore, as we gain some understanding of emptiness, we must resist any impulse to reify emptiness itself. To warn of this, Nagarjuna's *Fundamental Treatise* says,

> The Conqueror said that emptiness
> Eradicates all dogmatic views;
> As for those who take a dogmatic view of emptiness
> He said that they are incurable.

Some Tibetan and Western interpreters of the Madhyamaka tradition have taken this to mean that Madhyamaka is a radical form of skepticism in which the correct view (or perspective) is holding no view at all. In this reading, *any* sort of philosophical view or position is a dogmatic view that can be eradicated by seeing emptiness. Even holding that things are empty of intrinsic nature would then, it seems, be a dogmatic view.

Tsong-kha-pa disagrees: "A dogmatic view of emptiness does not mean taking the view that things are empty of intrinsic nature." The view that things are empty of intrinsic nature is the correct way to see things. It is the rare and precious understanding that will allow us to become free. Rather, a dogmatic view of emptiness is a view that reifies emptiness itself, failing to recognize that even emptiness is empty of any intrinsic nature. Having a dogmatic view of emptiness means thinking of emptiness as truly existent, viewing it as something special that exists in and of itself.

Why is it that, unlike Tsong-kha-pa, many insist on seeing Madhyamaka as a form of skepticism in which all views are bad? One reason has to do with ambiguous translations.[4] View (*lta ba*) is used in Tibetan to translate two very different words from Sanskrit, *drshti* and *darshana*. *Drshti* has the sense of dogmatic view, speculative view, bad view, or extreme opinion. It normally carries a negative connotation. *Darshana*, on the other hand, simply means philosophical view. Nagarjuna tells us that all *drshti*, not all *darshana*, are eradicated by emptiness. We need to have a philosophical view of emptiness (*shunyata-darshana*) that is not a dogmatic opinion (*drshti*). We need to have an understanding of emptiness that does not reify it. We need to have an understanding of ultimate reality that takes into account that even the ultimate reality exists only conventionally.

Another source of the "no views" reading of Madhyamaka is passages where Nagarjuna refutes the positions of (1) existence, (2) nonexistence, (3) both existence and nonexistence, and (4) neither existence nor nonexistence. This particular fourfold formula is sometimes called the tetralemma. Some Tibetans argue that the refutation of all four parts of the tetralemma means that reason refutes everything. The thrust of this argument is that there is no possible view or position about things that a Madhyamika can adopt, hold, and defend as her own.

As you might expect, Tsong-kha-pa disagrees with this reading. He explains that any reasonable interpretation of the tetralemma refutation needs to recognize that there is some implicit qualification. It defies reason to say that one can, without any qualification, refute both existence and nonexistence—in the same sense and without any qualifying words—with regard to the same subject. It is a contradiction. Moreover, supposing you did refute both existence and nonexistence, then how could you also refute the fourth position: that things neither exist nor do not exist? If you are refuting both existence and nonexistence, then that is the same as your saying that things neither exist nor do not exist. Tsong-kha-pa insists that it is pointless even to debate with someone who just stubbornly insists upon flagrant self-contradiction.

Intrinsically real things do not exist at all, even conventionally. On the other hand, mere things do exist inasmuch as they exist conventionally. There is nothing that exists ultimately because, as discussed above, there is nothing that can withstand reasoned analysis searching for the ultimate basis of its being. The Mad-hyamaka view, the middle way, is said to "avoid the extremes of existence and nonexistence," but that does not mean that Tsong-kha-pa literally refutes both that things exist and that they do not exist. He refutes any idea that things exist just as they appear to us now, as objectively real and naturally established. But they do exist interdependently, conventionally. He refutes any idea that tables and chairs are utterly nonexistent. But he accepts the utter nonexistence of intrinsically real things.

Tetralemma-like arguments arise at several places in Nagarjuna's work; Tsong-kha-pa points out that one must be careful about the meaning in each case. Are the things with regard to which the tetralemma is refuted "real things," that is, intrinsically existing things? Or are they mere things, conventionally existing? One way someone following Tsong-kha-pa could read the refutation of the tetralemma would be: We refute the reifying view that things exist ultimately; we refute the nihilistic view that things do not exist even conventionally; we refute that there is any single sense in which things both exist and do not exist; we refute that there is any single sense in which things neither exist nor do not exist.

Or we can say: We refute the view that things are intrinsically existent. We refute the view that things are intrinsically nonexistent. We refute the view that things are intrinsically both existent and nonexistent. We refute the view that things are intrinsically neither existent nor nonexistent. It is not in the essence of things to be or not to be, for things have no essential nature of their own. They are dependent arisings.

The Final Nature of Things

Tsong-kha-pa uses the word "nature" (rang bzhin) in several different senses. In a few places, it means the ordinary qualities of things, like the heat of fire, that allow our conventional wisdom to distinguish one thing from another. Very often, the term refers instead to an intrinsically existing nature, a naturally existing essence by virtue of which things can exist in and of themselves, on their own power. This is the object of negation. In fact, such a nature does not exist at all and through ignorantly conceiving of it, we are bound in cycles of suffering. Then again, in a third way, "nature" sometimes refers to the final or ultimate nature of all things, emptiness. In this sense, the (final) nature exists everywhere, always, as the sheer absence of intrinsic nature. Thus, the single word "nature" (*rang bzhin*) according to context can mean: (1) conventionally existing qualities (like the heat of fire), (2) something's objective existence by way of its own essence or nature (intrinsic being), and (3) the final and ultimate reality (emptiness).

Nagarjuna's *Fundamental Treatise* teaches that a nature is "something that is not fabricated and not dependent on another." A question arises as to whether at this point Nagarjuna is referring to intrinsic nature (which does not exist at all) or to the ultimate nature, ultimate reality, which is the absence of intrinsic nature. Chandrakirti explains that it is the latter. He writes:

> Is there a nature that has such qualifications as the master Nagarjuna claims? Yes, it is the "reality" of which the Bhagavan [Buddha] spoke extensively, saying, "Whether *tathagatas* [i.e., buddhas] appear or not, the reality of phenomena remains." . . . Does it exist or not? If it did not exist, for what purpose would bodhisattvas cultivate the path of the perfections? Why would bodhisattvas undergo hundreds of hardships in order to know reality?

Emptiness exists. It is not a metaphor or some other figure of speech. As the ultimate nature of reality, it is—as Nagarjuna says—"not fabricated." Tsong-kha-pa explains that this means that emptiness is not produced. It does not come into existence at some particular point in time without having existed before that. In other words, things have always been completely devoid of any ability to exist in and of themselves. They have always had this emptiness as their fundamental nature. Also, Nagarjuna says, the nature of reality *does not depend on something else,* some other thing or circumstance. Tsong-kha-pa explains that here Nagarjuna means only that emptiness, as the nature of things, is not something that arises or fails to arise contingent upon certain causes. Buddhas may or may not appear—that is, their appearance is in some way contingent on some circumstances. But this is not true of reality itself. The nature of reality is that things are necessarily empty and always empty and completely empty of any intrinsic being.

This idea that emptiness, as the final nature of reality, "does not depend on something else" might seem to imply that emptiness is the one existent that really does exist in and of itself. Everything else lacks intrinsic nature, but if emptiness exists without depending on causes or circumstances, then does that not mean that it exists independently? Must it not, therefore, exist by way of its own intrinsic power?

Tsong-kha-pa rejects this emphatically, stressing: "Even reality, the ultimate truth, has no intrinsic nature at all." He cites Chandrakirti as saying that this final nature is neither essentially existent nor essentially nonexistent. Rather, it "exists conventionally." Without emptiness, the Buddhist path would be senseless for there would be no liberating insight. On the other hand, if emptiness existed essentially, then when we took emptiness itself as the object of investigation, we should find that it does exist as its own essential nature. Instead we find that emptiness itself, like all other phenomena, is empty of any intrinsic or essential nature.

Although emptiness—as the ultimate nature—does not depend on causes or conditions, it still exists only in interdependence with other phenomena. For Tsong-kha-pa, emptiness—like all other phenomena—depends on the mind that recognizes it and knows, "Emptiness exists." Tsong-kha-pa describes how, when we first realize emptiness, it appears as an attribute of some other phenomena. Through reasoning, we come to understand, "This table is empty of intrinsic nature." While this is powerful and certain knowledge, it is mediated by a conceptual image of emptiness. We are not yet getting directly at the actual ultimate truth, emptiness itself. Later, along the path, the bodhisattva becomes very deeply familiar with emptiness in meditation that links analysis with serene one-pointed concentration. This culminates in the profound experience of direct, nondualistic mental perception of emptiness. For this ultimate mind, totally switched over to channel B (all emptiness radio), no conventional phenomena appear at all. This is what Tsong-kha-pa refers to as the actual ultimate truth. That is, the bodhisattva does not at that time think, "I am realizing emptiness," or "Oh, emptiness really does exist." *Only* emptiness appears.

Therefore, Tsong-kha-pa argues that emptiness can be recognized as the real nature of tables—or even as an existent—only from the perspective of some other mind, a conventional mind. Only a conventional mind that follows right in the wake of ultimate realization can look back on the profound experience of emptiness and know, "Emptiness exists; emptiness is the final truth." The fact of emptiness's existence is therefore established only by a conventional mind, albeit an extraordinary one.

Emptiness-of-Other

Tsong-kha-pa is concerned to refute one particular claim about ultimate truth, an idea associated with the "emptiness-of-other" teaching that had been popularized in Tibet by Shay-rap-gyal-tsen (1292–1361). As described by Tsong-kha-pa in his *Great Treatise*, this view holds that the ultimate exists on its own power, in and of itself. This profound and ultimate reality is not empty of its own nature; instead, it is empty in the sense that it is empty of other— conventional—things.

As Tsong-kha-pa describes this view:

> They accept that it is necessary to stop the conception of self, the root that binds all beings to cyclic existence. They

then assert that you do not stop the conception of self by realizing there is no intrinsic existence in what it apprehends as a self; rather, you stop it by knowing as truly existent some other unrelated phenomenon.

Although Shay-rap-gyal-tsen cites many sutras and tantras in support of his teaching, Tsong-kha-pa charges that this emptiness-of-other view is beyond the boundaries of any Buddhist scripture. To convey his sense of its absurdity, Tsong-kha-pa gives an analogy:

> Suppose that there is no snake in the east but someone thinks that there is and is terrified. You say to the distressed person, "You cannot stop your idea that there is a snake by thinking, 'In the east there is no snake at all.' Rather, you should think, 'There is a tree in the west.' This will stop your idea that there is a snake and end your distress."

The "tree in the west" represents the ultimate reality of the emptiness-of-other teaching. As Tsong-kha-pa sees it, meditating on this simply distracts us from—and does not at all address—our actual problem: the poisonous snake that is our reification of ourselves and the ordinary things around us. What we need to do, he says, is to use reason to attack and to eradicate the way that ignorance apprehends things as intrinsically real. It is this ignorance that binds us and other beings in cycles of misery. How could meditating on some other unrelated thing help us? He advises, therefore, that we stay clear of this type of teaching.

Whether we agree or disagree with Tsong-kha-pa's sharp comments on the emptiness-of-other view as he understood it, we can see how they are a natural outgrowth of his commitment to his core theme. We should take care to identify exactly how our minds exaggerate the reality of ourselves and other things. Then, relying on the texts of Nagarjuna, we must carefully refute these distortions, proving to ourselves that things are not as we have perceived and conceived them to be. Tsong-kha-pa tells us that there is no other path to liberation. We become free only through a process of analysis and subsequent realization of what we have analyzed. We will never discover any absolute truth or mystical experience that will absolve us of the need to do this work.

7. Intrinsic Nature*

Not Negating Enough

WHEN WE MADHYAMIKAS use reason to refute intrinsic nature, we say—to others and also to ourselves, within our own minds—things like this: "If school buildings existed by way of their own intrinsic nature, then they would not depend on causes or conditions." Or we may say, "If school buildings existed by way of their own intrinsic nature, then they would never change." These are good arguments against intrinsic nature because we can readily observe that things change and depend upon conditions, and these observations do contradict our idea that things exist in and of themselves.

However, we should not therefore conclude that the very meaning of emptiness—things' lack of intrinsic existence—is simply that things are impermanent or that things depend on causes. The idea that things are permanent and unchanging is a coarser misconception. It is easier to attack than the idea that things have their own intrinsic nature. We have to work our way down from things that are easier to understand to the deepest and subtlest object of negation.

To take another example: In addition to their causes, things also depend upon their parts. Each object that we apprehend can be mentally or physically analyzed, broken down into its component parts. Buildings are made of bricks, etc.; the bricks are made of

* Based on the *Great Treatise*, Volume 3, Chapters 16 and 17.

small fragments of rock; each of these fragments is made of billions of molecules; each of these molecules is made of much smaller atomic components. Do we ever arrive at some fundamental and irreducible particle or set of particles from which everything is built and which cannot be further analyzed into any kind of component?

Some Hinayana Buddhist philosophers say, "Yes, we do." They catalog the elemental particles and regard them alone as ultimately real, irreducible. Everything else—tables, etc.—they regard as conventional because these are just names we apply to reducible composites, collections of particles.

Along with other Mahayana Buddhist philosophers, Madhyamikas refute any notion of a partless particle. If an object takes up any space at all, then we can imagine its eastern and western sides. These two sides are parts, and the particle—no matter how small—is therefore not irreducible. It is a composite of its parts. On the other hand, if the particle occupies no space at all, then how can we ever use it to construct a composite thing like a table? Even if we have billions or trillions of particles, if each one takes up no space, we will never be able to build a visible and tangible object.

So, another argument Madhyamikas might make against intrinsic nature would be: "If school buildings existed by way of their own intrinsic nature, then they would not depend upon parts." It is easier to see that buildings depend on parts than it is to realize their emptiness! And depending on parts certainly contradicts the mistaken idea of something's existing in and of itself. But again: Simply knowing that something depends on parts is not the same as realizing its emptiness.

It is important to know very clearly that things change, depend on causes, and depend on parts. Such wisdom protects us from mistaken philosophies and undermines our tendencies to cling. But even more important is the fact that these understandings guide us toward the deeper and liberating truth that they imply: that all things are empty. We are not born with some idea of "partless particles" or "indivisible building blocks." Nor are we born with the idea of an uncaused divine Being who caused the world to exist. These ideas are acquired through culture; they are *not* the root source of our suffering in cyclic existence. They are simply branches or twigs that have grown, nourished from that root. If we only prune off some branches, new branches will grow.

Tsong-kha-pa is quite eloquent and forceful on this point. If all of our reflection and reasoning is aimed at refuting culturally acquired misconceptions associated with this or that religion or philosophy, then we are not getting down to the fundamental, innate ignorance that is the true basis of our misery. It would be quite absurd to say that someone became enlightened because they realized in meditation that there are no elemental particles, or that there is no divine creator. We are suffering because of a deeply rooted, pernicious, and pervasively influential misconception, the misconception that we exist by way of our own intrinsic natures. Like surgeons operating on ourselves, we have to use reason and meditation to cut out the deepest causes of our misery.

The Actual Object of Negation

That cars and tables, people and schools are devoid of any trace of analytically findable nature does not mean that they do not exist. Clearly they do exist. But what kind of existence can things have when they have no shred of existence from their own side? As we have seen, things exist as *dependent arisings*, phenomena that exist only through their interconnections with other (equally empty) phenomena.

Often we speak of dependent arising as though it were shorthand only for the dependence of effects upon causes and conditions. However, dependent arising also includes the idea that wholes depend upon their parts as well as the idea that *all things depend upon being designated or imputed by consciousnesses.* For example, fire arises in dependence upon fuel as a causal condition; but fuel is something that a mind identifies as burnable and on that basis thinks, "There is fuel." Likewise, cars are physically built up out of auto parts, but auto parts are recognized and imputed by the mind in consideration of their connection with real or potential cars. In Madhyamaka, the term "dependent arising" includes the notion that *all* things exist in dependence upon conceptual designation. In order to appreciate Tsong-kha-pa's position on intrinsic nature, we have to realize that it is *this* type of dependent arising that is most crucial. This is what we have to explore in order to identify the precise sense of "intrinsic nature" that is the deepest object of negation.

When we are careful not to negate too much or too little, what exactly is it that our reasoning about things finally refutes? Tsong-kha-pa identifies this actual object of negation as *things having their own way of existing without being posited through the force of consciousness.* This is what we mean by "self" or "intrinsic nature." The sheer absence of this is emptiness. Therefore, at bottom, to understand emptiness means understanding that things have no way of existing apart from minds that impute them.

This is difficult to understand, and we can see that it is not at all how we ordinarily perceive the world. In teaching this, I begin by scratching out a large letter A on the chalkboard. I ask the students what it is, and they say, "A." But where does this identity as an A come from? Does it come from the chalk dust? Does it come from the shape of the left slanted line? The right line? The centrally located crossbar? On the thin surface of the board, it is clear that there is no hidden interior place where the intrinsic A-ness of the A can reside. The A is something we ourselves are creating; it is an unspoken agreement to which we are parties. We ascribe, or impute, identity as A to a certain sort of shape. It is a matter of convention.

Once we recognize our involvement, it is important to notice that this process of ascribing is ongoing and unconscious. When we first look at the board, prior to analysis, there is a strong sense that we are seeing something that is out there, existing from its own side as an A. It seems as though it is radiating out, broadcasting clearly, the message of its "A" identity. We experience ourselves as passive receivers tuning in to a message that is being projected to us from the board.[5]

This sense is altered only when we begin to ask, "What is an A, really?" We find that an A utterly lacks any natural, independent identity from its own side, apart from our participation—but that it is, mysteriously, nonetheless fully capable of functioning. It works in words; it works as a letter-grade on a test. It does its job perfectly well even though it has no trace of the objective existence that we unconsciously attribute to it. This seems mysterious, even disconcerting, because we are deeply habituated to the idea that objective and intrinsic existence is necessary for things to be real and to work.

Another example that works in much the same way is money. A dollar bill pulled from my pocket at first looks like it is, quite objectively and independently, a real dollar. Some people feel—consciously or unconsciously—that when we talk about money, we are at last dealing with the fundamental reality of the world. Of course, like the letter A, dollars—and the paper or coins that carry dollar values—are all completely a matter of convention. Currency markets track the ever-shifting meaning of these conventions; there is no natural and objective value in dollars. But we can still spend them! Conventional reality works.[6]

Here is the example that Tsong-kha-pa uses: In the twilight someone sees a rope and mistakes it for a snake. Suppose we leave aside anything we might know about the perspective of the person who sees the snake. Instead, we will ask about what the snake is like on its *own* terms. This is absurd; we cannot begin to discuss the features of the snake because, in fact, there is no actual snake there at all. Analogously, suppose we leave aside any consideration of how people and cars and tables appear to ordinary, valid conventional consciousnesses, and ask, "How do these things exist from their own side? What are they like in and of themselves?" There is nothing that is purely objective, nothing out there completely apart from mind that we can pin down and point out.

Unlike the hallucinated snake, these people and cars do exist, but they do not at all exist on their own. However, they do not present their lack of independent existence to our senses; instead, they look as though they were established on their own, out there. The delusion that is the root of cyclic existence involves seeing things—particularly ourselves—as having just this sort of objective and autonomous being. This delusion sees things as being set up from their own side, as having their own natural way to be there. Tsong-kha-pa says that this ignorant mind "apprehends each phenomenon as having a manner of being such that it can be understood in and of itself, without being posited through the force of a conventional consciousness."

Whatever we know or talk about is already a thing-as-it-is-known, a thing as conceived by a mind. We cannot talk about or get at things as they are in and of themselves, apart from mind or in a way that is logically prior to any kind of conceptualization. For Tsong-kha-pa, this is because things have no nature in and of themselves, apart from mind. When we leave aside analysis of how things appear to our minds and attempt to analyze objects in and of themselves, we soon realize that there is nothing to which we can point. And it is not simply because we happen to be trapped in a situation where we cannot step out of our skin and take an objective view of the matter, the real thing in question. It is because the thing in question, that which we would wish to know, is already something of which we are conceiving, something that we are asking about. When we completely set aside the involvement of our minds, and ask about how things are in and of themselves, we never find a shred of thing-in-itself. *This* understanding, that things are empty in this way, is precisely the opposite of how ignorance sees things.

Mind and the World

We usually suppose that the world is already and always fully real, independent of our minds, out there waiting to be revealed by the searchlight of consciousness. In fact, our minds are actually collaborating in the creation of the world, moment by moment.

This does *not* mean that hallucinated snakes have the same status as people and cars and tables. Snakes falsely imputed to be ropes do not in fact exist, while tables and people do exist because they have a valid, conventional existence. This is a vitally important distinction. Suppose I very much want gold. I may see a rainbow and, affected by my desire for gold, think, "Over there I will find a pot of gold." This is rather in the nature of seeing a rope and, out of fear, believing it is a snake. There is no snake, no gold, in those places at all. But there is a rope; there is a rainbow. These things exist conventionally. We can appropriately impute them, saying, "There it is." They function.

Another way to make this clear is to consider the case of dreams. The objects that appear to our minds in dreams, under the influence of sleep, are not able to perform the functions that they appear to have. A dream cup does not hold functioning water; a dream gun does not shoot deadly bullets. The water and the bullets that appear in the dream cannot quench or kill. The dream mind to which a gun appears is impaired by sleep and is not a conventionally valid consciousness. Likewise, if my eyes are bad and I see two moons in the sky over the earth, I have not thereby created a second moon. Or, in the case of the letter A, if I look at the board and, without my glasses, think that it is an N, this certainly does not make it an N. On the other hand, when our unimpaired vision apprehends a certain shape that is the correct basis of imputation, then our minds think, "A." This is enough; that is all it takes for the letter to work in our language or in a school's grading system.

So we can recognize that this idea—that things depend upon minds—does not destroy conventional existence. At the same time, it is definitely not just another way of talking about what we already know. It does not leave our usual sense of the world unscathed. To take the snake example: When a person sees a rope and imagines a snake, there is no snake at all in the rope. But even when there actually is a snake and we perceive a snake, the snake as we perceive it is also *completely* absent. It is just as nonexistent as the rope-snake. This is profound and important to reflect upon. As we perceive it, the snake is inherently existent. It appears to our minds as something objectively real, existing in and of itself. Such a snake does not at all exist right now—and it never could exist. Thus, when we feel that Tsong-kha-pa's emphatic validation of conventional reality is pulling us too far in the direction of affirming the ordinary way that things appear, we can recall: snakes and ropes are *equally* devoid of the kind of snakes I perceive, believe in, and fear. Tables are utterly devoid of the kind of table that I believe in. People exist, but people just as I now conceive of them have *never* and could never exist even to the slightest degree.

Unlike some Buddhist systems, Tsong-kha-pa's Prasangika Madhyamaka system does assert that there is a fully functioning external world, a world that exists outside of our minds. However, in the same breath it emphasizes that this external world is utterly dependent upon consciousness. For example, when a god, a human, and a ghost each look at a bowl of fluid, the god sees nectar, the human sees water, and the ghost sees a mixture of pus and blood. Each being *correctly* perceives the fluid in accordance with the constitution of her respective sense and mental faculties. We cannot talk about what is *really* in the bowl apart from the correct perspective of the various perceivers. While some Buddhist systems use this example to show that there are no external objects at all, Prasangika Madhyamaka holds that the nectar, blood, and water do exist externally, but only in dependence upon the minds ascribing them. All three fluids can be simultaneously present, unmixed, in relation to diverse but correct perspectives.

When I teach this, sometimes I point out the tiny spiders clinging to the corners of the room. We are present together with them, here and now. We each have healthy minds and sense faculties. Our perceptions of the immediate environment are both correct, and yet they are so radically different as to be mutually incomprehensible. Which of us sees what is *really* there?

Or think about taking a dog for a walk. Going down the street
ther, there is only a partial overlap between the dog's valid

perceptions and my valid perceptions. We living beings all inhabit functioning worlds that arise through the unimpaired operation of our respective mental and sensory faculties; these worlds are external to—but never independent of—our minds. Thus it is that the worlds of our experience intersect and overlap in astonishing ways, in infinitely complex patterns. All of this would be completely impossible if in fact each thing actually existed objectively, out there on its own, by way of its independent and intrinsic nature.

8. The Two Types of Madhyamaka*

CAN YOU BELIEVE your eyes? Do your senses give you a clear picture of the world as it is? Some think that our senses mirror the world, but that we lose touch with reality and fall into misery as we build up distorted conceptualizations about our experiences and then become entangled by our emotional reactions to these conceptualizations. Others, including Tsong-kha-pa, say that the problem is deeper still. Our senses have already misrepresented the world even before our thoughts take hold of these images, even before we react to them with anger or desire.

As we have seen, Tsong-kha-pa constantly champions the *validity* of the information we get from our unimpaired senses about conventional things. At the very same time, however, he insists that these valid sense consciousnesses are mistaken about *how* conventional things exist. They misperceive things as having their own intrinsic nature. Things appear to them as though they were established objectively, independently, from their own side. Our mental consciousnesses often—but not always—actively assent to this false appearance, conceiving of things as existing in an exaggerated way, existing in and of themselves. This kind of mental delusion is the root of our suffering. It becomes especially prominent when we have strong afflictive emotions such as greed, jealousy, anger, envy, hatred, and pride.

* Based on the *Great Treatise*, Volume 3, Chapters 17–20.

A key message of Tsong-kha-pa's discussion of the two types of Madhyamaka is that conventional sense experience gives *valid* knowledge of its object, but is nonetheless *mistaken* about how its object exists. All Madhyamikas agree that intrinsic nature appears to our senses, but cannot be found upon ultimate analysis. On Tsong-kha-pa's reading, Svatantrikas (like Bhavaviveka) are those Madhyamikas who accept that, at a conventional level, things actually do have intrinsic nature just as they are perceived. To exist at all entails having intrinsic existence. However, since there is nothing that holds up under ultimate analysis, everything is ultimately empty. Emptiness is the lack of *ultimate* existence.

Prasangika Madhyamikas such as Chandrakirti, on the other hand, are those who say that even our healthy senses are persistently mistaken in one regard: the appearance of things as having intrinsic nature is false, *even conventionally*. People and cars exist conventionally, but intrinsic nature does not exist at all. Emptiness is the absence of intrinsic nature. For Prasangikas, this means the same thing as the lack of ultimate existence because, in their view, if things *did* have intrinsic nature, that nature would have to be found under ultimate analysis. The impossibility of finding things when one searches out how it is that they ultimately exist means that they have no essential nature at all. And yet, they exist and function.

It is important to recognize that one does *not* find direct, unambiguous statements about this difference between Prasangika and Svatantrika in the Indian Madhyamaka texts. Moreover, the earlier Tibetan scholars who first classified Madhyamikas as Prasangikas and Svatantrikas did not notice any philosophical difference in their views of ultimate reality. This was something Tsong-kha-pa discovered, inferring it from his close reading of the Indian texts.

Originally, Madhyamikas were classified as Prasangika or Svatantrika based not on their understanding of emptiness but on how they use reason to induce understanding of emptiness. Svatantrikas such as Bhavaviveka insist on using autonomous syllogisms (*svatantra*) to attack wrong views. In convincing others about emptiness, they insist upon arguments that are—or can be converted into—positive assertions that are formally correct in terms of traditional Buddhist logic. Prasangikas such as Chandrakirti, on the other hand, are comfortable attacking wrong views with contradictory consequences (*prasanga*), which are *reductio ad absurdum* arguments. This means that Prasangikas often use arguments that—without necessarily implying a specific alternative position—draw out contradictions implied by the position of the person whose views they are critiquing.

Tsong-kha-pa argues that Bhavaviveka's insistence on autonomous syllogisms is not just a difference in method but also evidences an underlying difference—a shortcoming—in his view of emptiness. The discussion of these points in the *Great Treatise* is famous as the most difficult portion of the text. Here, I simply offer a summary explanation of Tsong-kha-pa's conclusions.

In order to understand emptiness, you do not necessarily have to understand or agree with Tsong-kha-pa's argument about how Bhavaviveka betrays his belief in intrinsic nature. Nor do you have to be absolutely sure that Bhavaviveka really held the position Tsong-kha-pa claims to have discovered implicit in his arguments. Our purpose is to understand emptiness; it is not to debate the details of Buddhist intellectual history. For us, this controversy over how to reason about reality is an opportunity to become more familiar with Tsong-kha-pa's view of emptiness itself.

The Background

As Tsong-kha-pa relates, Nagarjuna's *Fundamental Treatise* opens with a refutation of reified production, a denial that things are ever produced from themselves, from intrinsically other things, from both, or without any cause. Commenting on this, the scholar Buddhapalita explicates Nagarjuna by pointing out the faults of the other systems in which each of these positions about production is held. For example, there is the case of the non-Buddhist Samkhya philosophers of India who say that things are, in a sense, produced from themselves because they arise from already existing, nonmanifest forms of themselves. In response, Buddhapalita gives the *reductio ad absurdum* argument, "It absurdly follows that production of the same thing over and over again must be endless because, as you say, things arise from themselves."

Thereafter, Bhavaviveka wrote a commentary on Nagarjuna, criticizing Buddhapalita. He points out that Buddhapalita's *reductio ad absurdum* arguments are simply fallacies internal to the other systems' positions. They cannot be readily converted into positive assertions that will prove the Madhyamaka position using sources of knowledge acceptable to both parties. And this is precisely what Bhavaviveka thinks is properly required. As a logician, Bhavaviveka feels compelled to take issue with the way Buddhapalita's commentary deviates from the then-established standards of formal logic. Bhavaviveka does not at all fault Nagarjuna; he takes it that Buddhapalita has misinterpreted Nagarjuna. He sets out to show how Nagarjuna's arguments *can* be formulated as self-standing proofs, autonomous arguments for the correct position that there is no ultimately existent production.

Subsequently, Chandrakirti wrote his own commentary on Nagarjuna, siding with Buddhapalita in the face of Bhavaviveka's critique. In brief, Chandrakirti criticizes Bhavaviveka's use of autonomous syllogisms. In defense of Buddhapalita, he argues that it is proper for Madhyamikas to debate about emptiness using *reductio ad absurdum* arguments, arguments that draw out internal contradictions in the position of the other party. This is the defining moment for the distinction between the two types of Madhyamaka.

Tsong-kha-pa's Explanation

For ease of explanation, let's make up our own syllogism: "The table is empty of existing in an ultimate sense because it is a dependent arising." Table is the subject of the syllogism. The major premise (known in Buddhist logic as the "entailment" or "pervasion") is that *whatever is a dependent arising must be empty of existing in an ultimate sense*. The minor premise (known as the "presence of the reason in the subject") is that *a table is a dependent arising*. The thesis being proven, the *probandum*, is that *the table is empty of existing in an ultimate sense*.

Roughly speaking, this kind of direct syllogism is the form of argument Bhavaviveka insists that we as Madhyamikas must make to non-Madhyamikas. Indeed, Tsong-kha-pa says that we *could* make arguments in this form. Our syllogism is an argument that Tsong-kha-pa accepts and that he will advance to someone who is ready to understand it. On the other hand, it is problematic to *insist* on this formulation—as Bhavaviveka does in criticizing Buddhapalita—for it is unlikely that this kind of argument will be especially persuasive at the outset. This is because our non-Madhyamika friends are proponents of true existence. For them, things exist as they appear. They take it that their empirical knowledge of a table includes authoritative confirmation of the intrinsic nature of the table. They take it as given that things have their own essential nature and on that account exist in an ultimate sense. It is therefore highly unlikely that they will be readily moved to adopt our Madhyamaka thesis.

Rather than baldly stating to non-Madhyamikas a thesis that directly contradicts what they take to be absolutely certain, Chandrakirti (and Buddhapalita) indicate a way to prepare the opponents gradually by first pointing out contradictory consequences attendant to their position. We might say, "Things must never change because, as you say, they exist through the power of their own essential nature, not depending on any other circumstances or conditions." Eventually, when their certainty about intrinsic nature has been greatly weakened, we Madhyamikas may have success in stating our thesis directly to them. This is how Tsong-kha-pa understands the Prasangika method of reasoning.

But Tsong-kha-pa goes beyond this point to ask, "What does it mean that Bhavaviveka, a brilliant scholar, fails to appreciate what Buddhapalita is doing?" For example, if we all agree to the same four premises, then we can state to one another direct arguments about what these premises imply. Likewise, if we all agree to the same empirical data, then we can argue about what conclusions to draw from these perceptions. But suppose the other party accepts only three of our four premises and also takes it as given that the same mind that validates the first three premises simultaneously confirms the exact opposite of our fourth premise. The possibilities for straightforward debate are now much more constrained. In such a case, our most effective means of persuasion cannot be to state baldly our fourth premise as a thesis. Its falseness seems obvious to the other party. Our best course is to begin reasoning in an indirect manner, pointing out internal contradictions that we find implied by our opponent's view.

This is something that Bhavaviveka, famous as a great logician, must have understood. Therefore, Tsong-kha-pa says, by *insisting* that we Madhyamikas must prove emptiness by stating an autonomous syllogism directly to non-Madhyamikas, Bhavaviveka implies that Madhyamikas are in fact debating with non-Madhyamikas from a shared empirical knowledge base, some common understanding of *how* things exist at the conventional level. That is, Bhavaviveka must think that the only difference between Madhyamikas and non-Madhyamikas is that we have analyzed more deeply and worked out the correct implications of the common body of empirical evidence upon which all agree. In this way, Tsong-kha-pa argues, Bhavaviveka implies that intrinsic nature, just as it appears to our ordinary senses, does in fact exist conventionally.

Courtroom Analogy

Suppose that there has been a serious traffic accident, with personal injuries. We Madhyamikas are the prosecution team, arguing for the conviction of the man who caused the accident by running a red light. An eyewitness comes forward to present an impartial account of the accident. I know that the witness, while strictly honest, is also completely color-blind. His testimony about the color of the light at the time of the accident, crucial to the case, is simply mistaken. But as I watch my Madhyamika co-counsel conduct the cross-examination, I notice something odd. While he is working doggedly for a conviction, his line of questioning does not bring forward or take into account that the witness is completely color-blind. While he agrees with me that the accused is guilty, my co-counsel's mode of argumentation suggests that he shares with the defense an implicit assumption that all of the witness's evidence is fully reliable.

The traffic accident is analogous to the disaster of samsara; trying to get a conviction represents trying to discredit the conception that things exist in an ultimate sense—the delusion that causes samsara. The witness represents the testimony of our senses regarding tables, chairs, etc. Color blindness represents the inability to differentiate *existence* from *intrinsic existence*. My co-counsel is Bhavaviveka, who argues for a conviction in a manner that betrays his implicit and unspoken assumption—shared with the non-Madhyamika defense team—that the honest testimony from the witness of our senses must be trusted utterly.

Tsong-kha-pa Distinguishes Two Types of Madhyamaka

Bhavaviveka never directly asserts that he accepts intrinsic nature. Bhavaviveka's insistence on autonomous syllogisms is one key piece of evidence that Tsong-kha-pa uses to infer that Bhavaviveka accepts intrinsic nature and thus does not distinguish between existence and intrinsic existence. In the *Great Treatise*, Tsong-kha-pa also points out another piece of evidence: when Bhavaviveka talks about refuting essence or intrinsic nature, he adds the qualification "ultimately." Bhavaviveka tells us that intrinsic nature does not exist *ultimately*, or *under analysis*. Is he implying that it *does* exist conventionally? Considering all of the evidence, Tsong-kha-pa concludes that Bhavaviveka does imply this.

On Tsong-kha-pa's reading, Bhavaviveka's form of Madhyamaka

is one in which existence and intrinsic existence are tacitly assumed —though never explicitly asserted—to be one and the same. Existence/intrinsic existence does not hold up under the analytical pressure of Madhyamaka reasoning. But Bhavaviveka seems to believe that conventionally, without ultimate analysis, things *do* exist intrinsically—just as they appear to our healthy senses.

This discussion allows us a fuller understanding of how Tsong-kha-pa reads Chandrakirti's critique of autonomous syllogisms. The term "autonomous syllogism" (*svatantra*) does not just mean positive arguments that are backed up by valid knowledge of the subject and premises. It means arguments of this sort in which *the same sort of valid knowledge* is recognized by both parties as having confirmed the subject and premises. When Prasangika Madhyamikas debate with others, this is not possible because the others believe that the consciousnesses that know the subject and the premises are also, at the same time, implicitly confirming the *intrinsic nature* of these things. Thus Tsong-kha-pa, following Chandrakirti, rejects autonomous syllogisms precisely because he rejects the intrinsic nature that others take as implicitly confirmed in the process of establishing the subject and premises of an autonomous syllogism.

But this does not at all mean that Tsong-kha-pa and his followers never use syllogisms. Many earlier interpretations of Chandrakirti take his critique of Bhavaviveka as implying that Prasangikas never use syllogisms because they do not assert any thesis; they merely refute the positions of others. Tsong-kha-pa refutes these views at length, showing that we use syllogisms; we make positive assertions; we hold positions and argue for them. We seek to prove to ourselves and others that things are empty of intrinsic nature. We assert that things are dependent arisings. We do not differ from non-Prasangikas in the matter of whether we do or do not have a thesis.

Rather, we differ in that all of our Prasangika arguments are backed up by conventional and valid minds—knowledge of tables and so forth—that we recognize as being *mistaken* in the sense that their objects falsely appear to them as intrinsically existing. This is our kind of conventional valid cognition: a reliable witness as to *what* conventional things are present or absent, but one that constantly misperceives *how* these things exist. Non-Prasangikas do not accept, or even consider, this possibility. The falseness of the pervasive appearance of intrinsic nature is precisely what we are trying to prove to them. We know others do not accept this, so we do not assume that we can prove our position to them with direct arguments. It is analogous to the situation of trying to help someone deduce that the light was red via close cross-examination of the honest but color-blind witness. This is possible, but it is not to be achieved in a straightforward route.

Consider the syllogism: "The table is empty of intrinsic nature because it is a dependent arising." If a Prasangika states this to a person who believes that intrinsic nature is incontrovertibly known by the same mind that sees the table, then we have an immediate problem. Our disagreement—whether or not things have intrinsic nature—pertains to the accuracy of the raw data of sense observations, the very basis from which all of our inferential arguments need to develop. We think that our senses provide valid knowledge but are mistaken about intrinsic nature; the other person thinks valid knowledge of an object entails valid knowledge of that object's intrinsic nature. Because of this situation, followers of Chandrakirti must have recourse to *reductio ad absurdum* arguments in order to begin to persuade others.

Nonetheless, Tsong-kha-pa stresses, Prasangikas do accept and assert the position that the table is empty of intrinsic nature. This is our core thesis. Our aim is to be as effective as possible in helping others to accept this thesis and thereby to start on the path to spiritual freedom.

Concluding Comment

Against others such as Ha-shang, Tsong-kha-pa argues for the *validity* of sensory knowledge and for the crucial role of logical arguments based on this knowledge. But in explaining the two types of Madhyamaka, he balances this through his emphatic support for Chandrakirti's sharp critique of the logician Bhavaviveka. As Tsong-kha-pa reads the situation, Bhavaviveka's rigid stance on the formal workings of logic implies and reveals a subtle but crucial reification. By joining with Chandrakirti in refuting Bhavaviveka, Tsong-kha-pa shows how he can celebrate the power of analysis without straying to a reifying extreme. Conventional knowledge is valid but the accompanying appearance of intrinsic nature is mistaken. Therefore, logic still works, but some traditional rules for formulating arguments are not operative because they are founded on the assumption that valid minds get at the intrinsic nature of the object of debate.

Indirectly, Tsong-kha-pa's discussion of this issue buttresses his theme that conceptual thought is *not* the root source of our problems. Throughout the *Great Treatise*, Tsong-kha-pa makes this point by emphasizing the positive power of analysis, but in this discussion of Bhavaviveka he makes the complementary point that even direct sense experience, like conceptual thought, is mistaken about how things exist. If we build our practice on the idea that all conceptual thought is wrong, we may suppose that the goal is to "get back" to some pure, raw, preconceptual experience. In such a case, we will be getting back to a valid source of information—but one that nonetheless includes a mistaken aspect, a false appearance of intrinsic nature.

Therefore, if we work from the assumption that we can trust how things appear preconceptually, we will not negate enough. Things vividly appear, even to our unimpaired senses, as though they had their own intrinsic nature. Normally, we never question this appearance. Wisdom is the path of analytically challenging it and becoming certain that it is false.

9. Who Am I, Really?*

A Puzzle

NEAR THE OUTSET of her adventures in Wonderland, Alice asks, "I wonder if I've been changed in the night? Let me think: *was* I the same when I got up this morning? I almost think I can remember feeling a little different. But if I'm not the same, the next question is 'Who in the world am I?' Ah, *that's* the great puzzle!"[7] Alice then ponders whether she has been changed into her friend Ada, or else perhaps has had the misfortune to become her friend Mabel. For if she has been changed, she has indeed become someone else—and it might well be someone she knows!

Those who love and raise children experience the poignancy of their rapid transformation from baby to toddler, young child, adolescent, and then adult. Is the baby I rocked on my chest the same person as this young man? Or is this a different person? We may notice the same problem, and perhaps a similar poignancy, when we look at old photographs. Am I the same person as, or a different person from, the nine-year-old Guy in the photograph? It feels hard to give either answer.

If we are pressed to stay focused on this question and to give an answer, we quickly begin to get uncomfortable. Is it the same person or a different person? Our discomfort may cause us to change the subject, dismissing the teacher or the book that is pressing us

---

* Based mainly on the *Great Treatise*, Volume 3, Chapters 21 and 22.

to work out the "great puzzle" of who we are. Our discomfort is based on a profound dissonance between how things really are—flowing, ungraspable, intermingling—and how we usually think and talk about them—as discrete and autonomous concrete units. Meditating on emptiness means committing yourself to going deeper and deeper into that dissonance so that it intensifies and becomes almost unbearable—as though there were a small child screaming in your ear demanding to know: *Who* are you? How *do* things exist?[8]

Intrusive Elephants and Married Bachelors

Let's begin by summarizing the steps in meditative analysis. First, we must identify in introspective meditation our own conception of intrinsic nature. This false self is like a demon that has caused us infinite torment. We can lure the demon out into the light by imagining situations of righteous indignation, in which one has been falsely accused, and then watching like a spy from a corner of the mind, trying to observe just what one's sense of self is like at that time. Without some exercise like this, it is tough to catch ourselves in the act of self-reification. The point is that we must notice within our own experience the ignorance that is the root of our cyclic existence, our own misconception of ourselves as having intrinsic nature.

Then, we have to set before ourselves a limited but *comprehensive* set of alternatives for how such a nature might exist if it did, in fact, exist. As an analogy, suppose someone were suffering from the delusion that there was an elephant in the house. We could make a comprehensive list of all the rooms in the house, or perhaps a list of all the spaces in the house that might in any way be large enough to contain an elephant. Then we could ask the deluded person to set it very firmly in mind that, were there an elephant in the house, it would absolutely have to be in one of those rooms. If he had some doubt, then we could add more places to the list, even if they seemed logically unnecessary, until he was able to feel decisively confident that any elephant located in the house would *have* to be in one of those places.

Then, when a search of each room turned up no elephant, the force of his sense that, "There is simply nowhere else for an elephant to be" would be converted into the realization that, quite contrary to his delusion, there is no elephant in the house at all.

The case of the married bachelor is another analogy that, while superficially strange, gives us a picture of the analytical process as a whole. Suppose there is a person who is causing herself and others needless suffering, and suppose that at the back of these problems is her misconception that she will be happy only when she finds a married bachelor. We help her first to recognize that she has this misconception—to notice how this strange idea appears within her own mind. Then we consider the alternatives: the married bachelor must be either wed or unwed. When she has a strong sense of conviction that these two choices exhaust all possibilities, we can then rule out each of the alternatives through what appears to *us* to be ridiculously obvious analysis: he cannot be wed because he is a bachelor; he cannot be unwed because he is married. For someone who has been in the thrall of a harmful delusion, it is vital to work through each step carefully. This should allow her to see, with certainty, that she was grasping after something that is not there and never could exist at all.

While strange, this analogy has advantages over the elephant in the house. The analogy of the married bachelor illustrates how the process of analyzing intrinsic nature is a case of logically limiting alternatives and refuting each one. It is not a physical searching, as with the elephant. Moreover, while unlikely, it really is possible for there to be an elephant in the house; the married bachelor is impossible. It happens to be the case that there are no elephants in my house right now, and it may happen to be the case that unicorns have never existed anywhere. But—like the married bachelor—persons who exist in and of themselves, by way of their own essential natures, simply *cannot* exist, now or ever.

Analyzing a Chariot

Madhyamaka treatises include many different arguments refuting any essentialist view. In the *Great Treatise,* Tsong-kha-pa describes the process of meditative analysis of the intrinsic self of the person mainly in terms of one particular argument known as the lack of sameness and difference (*gcig du bral*). He first exemplifies how this argument works by analyzing a chariot and then applies the same argument to the person.

Tsong-kha-pa's explanation of the "lack of sameness and difference" begins by describing what has been known as the law of the excluded middle. It has sometimes been said, quite erroneously, that this principle is absent in non-Western logics. Sometimes we still encounter the perspective that Asian religions, or Buddhism in particular, are about mystical experience to the exclusion of rational analysis. Let's consider one of Tsong-kha-pa's statements of the excluded middle in the *Great Treatise:*[9]

> In the general case, we see in the world that when a phenomenon is mentally classified as accompanied, it is precluded from being unaccompanied, and when it is classified as unaccompanied, it is precluded from being accompanied. In general, therefore, same and different, as well as singular and plural, preclude any further alternative because the unaccompanied and the accompanied are [respectively] singular and plural.

In other words, accompanied and unaccompanied, like wed and unwed, are X and not-X. What is unaccompanied is alone, singular, and identical to itself. It is not diverse because it is one thing. What is accompanied is plural and diverse. So the basic principle that anything that exists must be either X or not-X entails that anything that exists must be either singular or plural, and must be either self-identical or diverse.

Tsong-kha-pa then uses this principle to limit the alternatives in the analysis of intrinsic nature:

> When you determine in the general case [that anything must be either] one or not one, then you will also determine that for the particular case [of something that exists essentially, it must be either] essentially one or essentially different.

So if a chariot, for example, had an essential or intrinsic nature, such would have to be demonstrated by rigorous analysis of whether it is identical to its parts or intrinsically different from them.

Is the chariot the same as its parts? No, for if it were, then just as the parts of a chariot are several and diverse, so the chariot too would be plural; or else, just as there is a single chariot there would only be one part. If the chariot were identical to its parts, then, since we say that a chariot *has* parts, the possessing agent would be identical to the possessed object. If agent and object could be identical in this way, then fire and fuel could just as well be identical. Simply putting a log (the burned object) in a cold fireplace should warm up the room because the burned object is the same as the burning agent, fire.

On the other hand, a chariot is not essentially separate from its parts because if it were, we would see cases of chariots appearing without any chariot parts, just as horses and cows can appear separately insofar as they are separate.

Since a chariot can be found neither among its parts nor essentially separate from them, it must lack an essential nature. This is because if there were an essentially existent chariot, it would have to be findable under this sort of analysis. The knowledge that things lack essential reality is a liberating insight into emptiness, the absence of intrinsic existence.

Another important point to note is that for Tsong-kha-pa the final basis for any argument, including this refutation of essential reality, is information provided by ordinary conventional consciousness. We see that a log is different from a flame, that a horse is different from a cow, that being accompanied is different from being unaccompanied. It is from this ordinary factual knowledge that we can develop arguments against essential nature. Our ordinary conventional consciousnesses are mistaken in that a log appears to them as though it were essentially real, but at the same time these conventional consciousnesses provide accurate and practical information. Not only can we use this information to light a fire—or select a car—but we also definitely need this information in order to form the argument against essential nature. As Tsong-kha-pa says, "Even when you analyze reality, the final basis for any critique derives from unimpaired conventional consciousnesses."

The Person

Tsong-kha-pa uses the same "absence of sameness and difference" argument to demonstrate that the self, or person, does not essentially exist because it is neither essentially one with nor essentially different from the mental and physical aggregates. He explains that the practitioner, having first identified the object of negation—the conception of an intrinsic self—in her own experience, then asks herself whether this essential self is the *same* as her mind and body or *different* from her mind and body.

The notion that the essential self is the same as the mind and body is contradicted by many arguments. Let's consider four of these: (1) it would be redundant even to speak of a self; (2) there would be many selves, or else only one aggregate; (3) the intrinsically existing self would be impermanent, arising and disintegrating; (4) any agent and its object could be identical.

If there were an essentially existing self that was exactly identical to the elements and aspects of the mind and body, then these aggregates would *be* that self. There would be no need to talk about it, conceive of it, or argue about it. The self would be simply and exactly a synonym for the mind/body complex. Yet in speech, reflecting our way of thinking, the self of a person seems very distinct from the person's mind and body. We use expressions like "my mind," "my body," "my hand," or "my feelings," or even "my life." How can the "me" that we think of as possessing these various and changing feelings be precisely the feelings themselves? Therefore, the essentially existent self cannot be identical to the mind and body.

The second argument is that if the aggregates of the mind and body were exactly identical to the essential self, then they would have to have all of the same qualities and attributes. For example, they would have to be numerically the same. Just as a person is conceived to have only *one* essential self, the aggregates of mind and body would then also have to be only one in number—whereas in fact, there are obviously many diverse parts of the mind and body. Or else, since these components are diverse, there would have to be many diverse essentially existing selves for each person. I would have ten "toe selves," and so forth. Yet this is not at all how it appears to us when we introspectively observe our sense of a "real self." This real self seems to be the singular essence and autonomous core of my being as a person. It is therefore contradictory to say that it is identical to the plural and diverse elements of mind and body.

The third argument is that if an intrinsically existing self were identical to the mind and body, then it would have to change moment by moment, just as the mind and body do. In that case, the intrinsically existing self of one moment would be different from the intrinsically existing self of a later moment. A consequence, then, of identifying the intrinsically existent self with the mind/body complex is that we would have to acknowledge that the essential self is different in each moment, as the body and mind change. But if the "me" of past moments is a different essence from the "me" of the present moment, then how can I remember things that the earlier person experienced? My former self was different *in essence*; it is essentially different from the "me" of this moment. And if persons who are essentially different can remember each other's experiences, then anyone in the world should be able to remember the experiences of any other person. Yet this does not occur.

A fourth argument is that if the intrinsic self were identical to the mind and body, then, since we say that a person *has* a body and *has* a mind, the possessing agent would be identical to the possessed object. If an agent and object could be identical in this way, then fire and fuel could just as easily be identical. As noted above, this would imply that putting a log in a cold fireplace should warm up the room, or that one could use a knife to cut itself.

But why should we not, then, consider that the intrinsically existing self is *different* from the mind and body? If the person had an essential character that was different from the essential character of the mental and physical aggregates, then my "self" could be found and identified quite apart from my mind and body. That is, just as horses and cows have different qualities and can be seen in different places, we should be able to point out my essential self in one place and time while my mind and body were somewhere else altogether.

In fact, we use the term "person" in reference to a continuum of changing mental and physical factors. The person, each of the individual factors of mind and body, and the whole continuum of ever-changing factors are all devoid of any essential or intrinsic nature. Because I have no essence, I am neither essentially the same as nor essentially different from Guy at age nine. I am also neither essentially the same as nor essentially different from persons with different mind-streams, such as George Bush. But unlike George Bush, I am in the same personal continuum with the Guy of yesterday and the Guy I was as a child. My experiences and choices at those times left imprints, like the footprints left behind by a bird that has now flown away. I inherit the effects of my own past actions. The choices we make create ripples, and from these our distinct but ever-changing set of inclinations and moral qualities roll down like a wave through the stream of our minds. So, conventionally, it is correct to say, "This is a picture of me when I was nine," and "That is not a picture of me; it is a picture of George Bush."

Tsong-kha-pa notes that non-Buddhist philosophies about an eternal and essential self arise when their proponents realize that the essential self really cannot be identical to the flux of mental and physical aggregates. Reaching the wrong inference, they then teach about the existence of a metaphysical self that is essentially different from the mind and body. However, their own ordinary and conventionally valid consciousnesses never perceive any essence or intrinsic self that is different from the mind and body. This is simply an imaginary construct. Instead of assuming that there *must* be a permanent self and then locating it as an essence distinct from the mind and body, they should realize that since an intrinsically existing self can be found neither as one with nor as different from the mind and body, it simply does not exist.

Since it is impossible for the person to be an essential self that is either one with or different from the aggregates, it is impossible for the person to have any essence. The person lacks any intrinsic nature. The person exists only nominally and conventionally, and yet is fully able to function as an agent on this basis. In order to make your understanding of this conclusion very solid, it is important to consider every way that suggests itself to your mind in which there might be an essential self lurking somewhere, slipping through the cracks. With careful and focused analysis, every possibility can be resolved into being a case of "same" or "different" and will then break down in light of fallacies such as those mentioned above.

In meditative practice, we cannot be content to work through one line of reasoning in an abbreviated form. We must use multiple lines of reasoning drawn from the treatises of Nagarjuna and other Madhyamikas, and we must feel ourselves being drawn deeply into the process of working through them again and again. Only in this way can we develop strong conviction that the intrinsic self to which we normally cling has never and could never exist at all.

Dependent Arising

The contradiction, the real case of the married bachelor, is that we cling to the illusion that things solidly exist in and of themselves, while at the same time we live in the midst of unrelenting evidence of how things are not only transient, but contingent upon other things as conditions. This is frighteningly similar to the delusion of the married bachelor in its implication that someone out there is both wed (related to another) and unwed (unrelated to another). Are things related to one another or not?

To us, it seems to be "common sense" that (1) things are real in and of themselves and (2) because they are real, they are able to be in relationships that connect them to other real things. I hear people articulate, and find within myself, thoughts that add up to this: If things were not *already real* before they hooked up with something else, then what would there be to hook together?

We are correct to intuit that there cannot be relationships without some related entities. Relationships do not exist apart from that which is related. However, we are profoundly wrong to believe that there must therefore be ultimately real things—unrelated and independent things—that just happen to be there on their own, and then later relate to one another.

Through meditating on how things are empty because they are dependent arisings, we retrain our minds to see that things exist *only* insofar as they are related to other things—none of which is ultimately real. Since nothing has its own way to set itself up, each and every thing is the expression of vast networks of relationships with and among other things. There is no bottom, no absolute ground of being, no unconditioned support or starting point. Everything emerges from the surging and relentless complexity of innumerable interdependent conditions, every one of which is analytically unlocatable.

Implicit in clichés such as "every snowflake is unique" is a celebration of our own uniqueness as living beings. The problem is only that we believe, usually unconsciously, that our uniqueness arises from an inner essence that is our private core. To defend and aggrandize that core, we harm others; to nurture that core, we build up our greed. We act as though malicious anger were our protective father, and craving were our sustaining mother. No one can begin to measure how much pain and anguish this has caused.

In fact, our uniqueness arises from our distinctive, ever-shifting, and infinite array of connections with other things. We are unique and important, but we do not *own* our uniqueness. We have no intrinsic core. We owe our uniqueness to all of our conditions—and to our emptiness. For without the open sky of emptiness, the rest of the world could not shine into and through us, and we could never be what we are—living beings making choices that matter.

Seeing Things as Like Illusions

How does the world appear to someone who has been doing this type of analysis in meditation? Tsong-kha-pa cites a poetic passage from the *King of Concentrations Sutra* teaching that all phenomena are like mirages, illusions, reflections, echoes, and dreams. He explains that in the case of conventional phenomena such as persons or forms, this means that there is an appearance of X, but one simultaneously understands that there is no intrinsically existent X present at all. It is like the case of a reflection, for example, where there may be a vivid appearance of a face, but we understand that there is in fact no face present in what is appearing.

At the end of analysis, when one emerges from meditation on emptiness, one discerns again the appearance of tables and chairs and persons. However, having just analyzed the emptiness of these things, they appear in a very different light. They seem illusion-like, perhaps vague, indistinct, or shimmering.

However, having an altered state of consciousness after meditation does not necessarily indicate that one has accurately realized how things are like illusions. As Tsong-kha-pa says, "That sort of experience comes to everyone who aspires to Madhyamaka tenets and hears a little of the teaching that shows that things lack intrinsic nature." He suggests that you may have this kind of experience even after meditation in which you have negated too much:

> When your analysis of an object uses reason to obliterate it, you first think, "It is not there." Then as you come to see the analyzer [yourself] in the same way, there is no one even to ascertain that nonexistence. So, with no way to determine what something is or is not, it begins to seem that what appears has become vague and indistinct.

Truly understanding the illusoriness of the person requires both a complete and accurate refutation of the person's intrinsic nature and an understanding that it is precisely these persons without intrinsic nature who engage in actions and experience their effects. In other words, the empty and illusory person *exists* and makes choices, acting effectively to help or to harm.

If you misidentify the object of negation even slightly and negate too much, then as your understanding of this "emptiness" strengthens, you undermine your confidence in the practice of virtues such as generosity, ethical discipline, and patience. Truly finding the Madhyamaka view requires understanding emptiness accurately, which is to say, understanding it in such a manner as to preserve its complete compatibility with dependent arising. Truly knowing emptiness is not, then, an encounter with meaninglessness. It is precisely what allows us to see with full assurance that our actions matter, that what we do will make a difference by serving as a condition for what will happen in the future.

Reminding us that finding this perspective is a great challenge, Tsong-kha-pa gives clear guidance on how to proceed:

> Form a clear concept of the object that reason will be refuting. Then focus on how, if there were such an intrinsically existing person, it could only be one with or different

from its aggregates, and how reason contradicts both of these positions. Develop certainty in seeing this critique. Finally, solidify your certainty that the person does not even slightly exist intrinsically. In the phase of meditating on emptiness, practice this often.

Then, bring to mind the conventional person who is undeniably apparent. Turn your mind to dependent arising, wherein that person is posited as the accumulator of karma and experiencer of effects, and be certain about how dependent arising is possible without intrinsic existence. When they seem contradictory, think about how they are not contradictory, taking an example such as a reflection.

When it seems to us that the person's emptiness of intrinsic nature contradicts the person's ability to act and to experience the effects of action, then Tsong-kha-pa invites us to use a reflection or a similar analogy to develop confidence in the complete compatibility of these two things. He then lays out exactly how this analogy works:

> A reflection of a face is undeniably a conjunction of (1) being empty of the eyes, ears, and such that appear therein and (2) being produced in dependence upon a mirror and a face, while disintegrating when certain of these conditions are gone. Likewise, the person lacks even a particle of intrinsic nature, but is the accumulator of karma and the experiencer of effects, and is produced in dependence upon earlier karma and afflictions.

A person appears very vividly to have intrinsic nature, just as the reflection of a face may appear very vividly to be a face. If we come upon a reflection of ourselves unexpectedly, in a very clean mirror, we may for a moment be startled. We may feel strongly that we are seeing another person. While this appearance as a person is completely false, the reflection does exist and does function effectively as what it actually is. It arises, functions, and passes away depending upon conditions.

Likewise, the person is completely devoid of any shred of the intrinsically existent nature that vividly appears to our minds. Such a nature is unfindable because of being utterly nonexistent, just as there is no actual person in the mirror. On the other hand, just as a reflection does exist as a mere reflection, a person does exist as a mere person. And, as it turns out, that is exactly the kind of person one needs to be in order to make choices, to act and to change, and to bring help to the world.

The *King of Concentrations Sutra* says:

> When reflections of the moon appear at night in clear, clean water, they are empty and ungraspable. Know that all phenomena are this way.
>
> A person tormented by thirst, traveling at midday in summer, sees mirages as pools of water. Know that all phenomena are this way.
>
> Although water does not exist in a mirage at all, a deluded being wants to drink it. Know that all phenomena are this way.

The Buddha is not a God issuing the great commandment: Do not grasp. Nor is he a judge who stands ready to condemn those who violate this commandment. Rather, the Buddha is our spiritual physician, giving us healthy advice. If happiness could be attained by grasping things, there would no need for Buddhism. All of our needless miseries arise because we continue to grasp after things that are in fact completely ungraspable—because they have no pith, no innermost core, no fixed essence.

What is true of chariots and persons is true of all things, and to the same degree. The Buddha points out the painful and sad futility of our clinging to objects, people, ideas, experiences, and identities that simply *cannot* be held, no matter how tightly they are grasped. Because they have no ability to set themselves up and exist on their own, we and the things around us are in flux, changing as conditions change. With no essential nature, neither our own selves nor the things around us have any inner handle by which we can grab and hold them. We are afraid to face this lack, this emptiness. Our fear arises from and feeds our grasping, and in this way we build a prison for ourselves, moment by moment. Yet by bravely facing the reality of emptiness, we can let go of our fear, anger, and greed. We can be free.

10. From Analysis to Insight*

Insight Requires Analysis

TSONG-KHA-PA INSISTS that nondualistic insight into the nature of reality must be founded upon careful and thoughtful *analysis* of how things exist. He cites a sutra that describes how a bodhisattva's insight—while based in a one-pointed concentration—is itself an analytical, differentiating mind:

> Regard inwardly and with discernment the mental image which is the domain of the meditative concentration on the topics upon which you have reflected . . . [A]ny differentiation of the meaning of these topics, or . . . thorough analysis, . . . view, or thought is called "insight."

Tsong-kha-pa retells a traditional story in which the Chinese master Ha-shang Mahayana—having seen this statement that meditative insight involves things such as analysis and differentiation—exclaimed, "I don't know how this can be a sutra!" In frustration, Ha-shang then kicked the text.

According to traditional Tibetan accounts, the Chinese monk Ha-shang Mahayana was the loser in a late eighth-century debate to determine whether Tibet would follow Buddhist teachings arriving from India or those from China. Ha-shang simply could

---

* Based on the *Great Treatise*, Volume 3, Chapters 25–27.

not believe that any sutra could identify meditative insight with analysis because it was his conviction that any kind of conceptualization whatsoever is a distorting reification. To find liberation, he taught, we should dispense with all analytical thought and meditate on reality by not bringing anything to mind.

Throughout the *Great Treatise*, Ha-shang functions as a stock character representing this perspective. Tsong-kha-pa argues (Volume 3, page 16) that this wrong-headed approach will leave Ha-shang and anyone who is like-minded with a great many sutras to kick. The *Cloud of Jewels Sutra* says,

> Serenity is one-pointed attention; insight is proper discernment. On the basis of genuine concentration, stabilizing your mind is serenity and the wisdom that differentiates phenomena is insight.

Thus, the liberating insight that will set us on the path to freedom is not a "spacing out" or "emptying the mind." It is a precise, rigorous meditative analysis that breaks through false appearances.

Tsong-kha-pa reports that the Indian scholar Kamalashila refuted Ha-shang in debate with an extremely apt citation from the *King of Concentrations Sutra*:

> If you analytically discern the lack of self in phenomena
> And if you cultivate that very analysis in meditation,
> This will cause the result, attainment of nirvana;
> There is no peace through any other means.

Kamalashila argues,

> If you say that you should not think about anything, you abandon the wisdom which has the nature of correct analytical discrimination. The root of sublime wisdom is correct analytical discrimination.

Withdrawal Is Not Enough

There is a very large gap between, on the one hand, analytical reasonings such as those described in the previous chapter and, on the other hand, the bodhisattva's direct, nondualistic experience of emptiness in nirvana. It is clear that Ha-shang is not the only one who sees this as an unbridgeable gap; he is simply a character deployed to epitomize an extreme form of that opinion. It seems that long after Ha-shang, even in Tsong-kha-pa's day and down to the present, there have been Tibetans teaching that because enlightenment is nondualistic and nonconceptual, our practice should from the very outset emulate that condition to the maximum degree. In their perspective, any practice that involves analytically searching for a philosophical understanding of reality will only bring about further entanglements in discursive and dualistic thought. Thus, we should instead stabilize our minds in a state completely free from any thought. They argue that setting the mind in a condition where it apprehends no object at all brings it into alignment with the ultimate reality because nothing exists in the face of emptiness.

Tsong-kha-pa is intent upon refuting this approach in any of its variations. Has this meditator who is setting his mind without any thought first understood the idea that this objectless condition will harmonize his mind with ultimate reality? If so, Tsong-kha-pa says, then he has in fact studied and adopted a philosophical view—the nonexistence of everything—and then meditated in accordance with that. So it is not really the case that he is doing no analysis. Rather, he has instead made an error in his analysis and negated too much.

That no object is found "in the face of emptiness" is true in the sense that when one searches for anything with ultimate analysis, it is not found. However, this does not at all mean that the mind of ultimate wisdom has no object of realization. It realizes emptiness, the utter absence of intrinsic nature. As discussed above, emptiness exists. It is fully compatible with dependent arising and all conventional truths.

In response, these teachers simply insist that all conceptual thoughts—about emptiness or anything else—are fraught with dualistic reification and on that account bind us in cyclic existence. They do not distinguish between correct thoughts and incorrect thoughts because all thinking is dualistic and brings about further reification. Liberation is attained by setting the mind in a state of nonconceptual suspension.

In addition to showing that this contradicts scriptures such as those cited above, Tsong-kha-pa reiterates an argument Kamalashila used against Ha-shang: This would make it impossible to practice generosity, compassion, nonviolence, and many other aspects of the Mahayana path. The cultivation of these virtues, critical to the bodhisattva path as described in many scriptures, requires that one consider other beings and their needs. As noted above in Chapter Three, perfect enlightenment is attained through a synergy of practices of wisdom and practices of virtue for developing merit. If one holds that wisdom cancels out any thoughtful engagement with other living beings, then one cannot develop the virtues of an enlightened buddha.

One version of the "no thought" teaching compares the discursive, conceptual mind as it goes out after its object to throwing a ball. After a thought reaches out to its object, we could then use analysis to chase after the mind's dualistic elaborations and try to run them down, like a dog chasing after a ball. But it would be better to stop the mind before it goes out after its object—like a dog jumping up to snatch a ball before it can be thrown. On this view, "those who train in scriptures and reasonings that determine the view" are devotees of an inferior practice that does not get at ultimate reality because it does not attack the problem right at its source—the mind's endless elaboration of dualistic concepts.

Of course, Tsong-kha-pa argues that the problem is not conceptual thought *per se*, but the gravely mistaken reification of objects as intrinsically existent. The influence of this *particular* misconception is present in both ordinary perception and ordinary thought, but the error itself is one that can and must be refuted by careful reasoning based on definitive scriptures.

Tsong-kha-pa acknowledges that those who hold their minds in nonconceptual states do not, at that time, think of things as intrinsically existent. On the other hand, they also do not realize that intrinsic existence is false. Therefore, they are not practicing a path that will liberate them. When they emerge from meditation, they will soon fall back under the spell of the *still-unrefuted* misconception of intrinsic existence. Referring to the intrinsically existent self of persons and the intrinsically existent self of other phenomena, Tsong-kha-pa advises,

> You must distinguish between (1) *not thinking about true existence* or the existence of the two selves and (2) *knowing the lack of true existence* or the nonexistence of the two selves. Remember this critical point.

Not thinking about a problem is not enough. We must know the truth.

If simply withdrawing the mind from thought were a path to liberation, then people would become buddhas just by fainting or falling deeply asleep. Teachers could use a quick upper-cut to the jaw in order to induce a supposed "objectless" awareness in students. But suspending all thinking is just like burying your head in the sand or closing your eyes in the face of danger.

Rather than living in denial, we have to confront our mistaken way of thinking, challenging it directly by using analysis to become absolutely certain that it is wrong. The buddhas are called "conquerors" because they have faced the enemy of ignorance and defeated it utterly with the weapon of analytical wisdom. Withdrawing from all thought is not only cowardly but ultimately futile and self-defeating.

Serenity on the Path of Wisdom

The initial realization of emptiness is a profound certainty arrived at through the analytical, introspective meditative process we have described. While it is a very powerful experience, it is a conceptual and therefore dualistic understanding. Nirvana is attained only through a direct, nonconceptual, nondualistic experience of emptiness. How can one get from one to the other?

In order to begin to refine a conceptual and thus dualistic understanding of emptiness into a liberating nondualistic experience, the bodhisattva uses the power of *serenity*, a powerful concentration developed through stabilizing meditation. Serenity is a state in which the mind and body have become pliant as the mind focuses firmly and one-pointedly upon its object. One-pointed absorption on a single object of concentration weakens the ordinary dualistic sense of subject and object. Pliancy means that your mind and body are serviceable, responsive. There is no resistance to practice. You take delight in focusing your mind on a virtuous object, while your body feels light and buoyant (Volume 3: 81–84).

To develop serenity, you use mindfulness (keeping your attention on an object) and vigilance (watching carefully to see when attention begins to slip) to focus your mind and to maintain attention continuously and clearly, without distraction. Eventually, the mind stabilizes, resting naturally where you have set it. When this practice develops to the point that your body and mind are pliant and blissful, then you have attained serenity. The Tibetan term for serenity (*zhi gnas*) suggests a *quieting* (*zhi*) of mental movement toward distracting external objects and *abiding* (*gnas*) on an internal object of meditation.

Bodhisattvas definitely must learn to focus their minds in this way. This is what creates the mental power that allows them *to begin* to progress from discursive analysis of reality to direct, nondualistic realization. Having attained serenity with regard to any object, and having separately realized emptiness through analysis, the bodhisattva then learns to make emptiness itself, the conclusion established in analysis, the object of serene attention. Serenity focused on emptiness is itself still a conceptual mind. This is because emptiness, having been realized through inferential analysis, presents itself to the bodhisattva's mind as a conceptual image. It is this image/idea of emptiness that is then taken as the meditative focal point for serenity.

Preparing for Insight

It is possible that one may analyze and even realize emptiness first, and then set out to attain serenity; it is also possible that one may attain serenity without yet having realized emptiness. In either case, one must *not* do extensive analytical meditation while working to achieve serenity for the first time. This is because the discursive movement of the mind from object to object as it analyzes is quite different from the nondiscursive stability of serene concentration on a single object. Tsong-kha-pa says,

> It is impossible to achieve serenity if, prior to achieving insight, you repeatedly alternate between analysis and post-analytic stabilization . . .

However, once serenity has been attained, one must return to the practice of analytical meditation, working again and again through reasonings demonstrating that all things are empty of intrinsic nature.

Tsong-kha-pa emphasizes that you *cannot* develop true insight simply by realizing emptiness once in analysis and thereafter practicing only serenity meditations in which you stabilize your mind on that conclusion. Rather, you have to *sustain* your understanding of emptiness by repeatedly returning to analysis, using multiple lines of reasoning, and working through them again and again. In this way, you become deeply accustomed to the certain knowledge that things are empty. Tsong-kha-pa says, "Ascertainment of the view becomes strong, long-lasting, clear, and steady to

the extent one becomes accustomed to what one has determined."
Insight is impossible if emptiness is something that you analyzed
one time and then only remember having realized. Tsong-kha-pa
says,

> When you have determined [the view of emptiness], you
> *repeatedly* analyze it using discriminating wisdom. Sta-
> bilizing meditation alone, without sustaining the view,
> will not create insight. Therefore, when you meditate
> after having attained serenity, you must sustain the view
> through continued analysis.

It is especially important to Tsong-kha-pa to emphasize that discerning analysis is a critical and continuing part of a practitioner's
meditation practice. It is not something that one does just at the
beginning, until one can attain serenity focused upon emptiness.
He shows that this point is supported by the treatises of Kamalashila, Chandrakirti, Bhavaviveka, and Shantideva. For example,
Bhavaviveka explains meditation on emptiness as an inquiry into
how things exist that is built upon the foundation of a previously
attained mental stability: "*After* your mind is set in equipoise, this
is how wisdom investigates . . ." This does not at all mean that
there is no analysis of emptiness before one attains serenity—
clearly, there is. However, it emphasizes the importance of *continuing* analysis even after serenity has been achieved. The order
of the six perfections, with meditative stabilization preceding wisdom, also reinforces this key point.

On the other hand, it will not work to do *only* analytical meditation after attaining serenity. Just as the force of your certainty
about emptiness will weaken if it is not sustained by repeated analysis, the strength of your serenity will degrade if it is not refreshed
with the repeated practice of stabilizing meditation. Therefore,
you must alternate between the practice of stabilizing meditation,
reinforcing your serenity, and analytical meditation, building up

your wisdom. This is the path leading to sublime insight. Tsong-kha-pa advises us,

> You alternate (1) developing certainty, profound certainty, that there is not even a particle of true existence in any thing or nonthing whatsoever, and (2) stabilizing your mind on the conclusion thereby reached.

One has to strike a balance between serenity and analysis, two kinds of practice that are superficially discordant. Analysis is required to see into the nature of things, but too much analysis weakens the mind's stability. Serene stability is required to give the mind focused power, but one cannot afford to become so absorbed in one's object that one forgets to use analysis to renew the certainty of one's conclusions about the nature of reality. Kamalashila explains that when too much analysis weakens one's serenity, the mind is like a flame placed in the wind. It wavers, becoming unfocused, so that it does not see reality clearly. On the other hand, if one practices too much serenity focused on emptiness, but does not refresh one's certainty about emptiness with more analysis, then one "will not see reality very clearly, like a person who is asleep." That is, the stability of the mind is strong, but the clarity of the object, emptiness, is weakening due to not being refreshed with more analysis.

Insight

Eventually, after long practice, the bodhisattva's analytical wisdom itself spontaneously *induces* the blissful and pliant condition of serenity. The term "insight" (*lhag mthong*) refers to an analytical wisdom that—in the same session of meditation and without interruption or effort—brings about serenity focused upon the object one is analyzing. Literally, insight (*lhag mthong*) means a *superior* or *special* (*lhag pa*) kind of *seeing* (*mthong*). This practice in which profound analytical insight naturally gives rise to serenity is called *the union of serenity and insight*.

The union of serenity and insight is a fusion of analytical power and sublime one-pointed focus. It is a mind that powerfully and analytically discerns its object without in any way fluctuating from pliant and one-pointed absorption. Tsong-kha-pa says that one should *not* think of it as "a small fish moving beneath still water without disturbing it." This striking image suggests that some Tibetans explained the union of serenity and insight as a composite mental state in which just a small portion of the mind engaged in penetrating analysis of ultimate reality without disturbing a vast ocean of mental peace. In contrast, Tsong-kha-pa sees it as a fully empowered and activated analytical mind, penetrating its object with serene and laserlike focus.

Analytical wisdom is called *insight* only at the point where it is able to induce serenity. Prior to that point, deep analytical wisdom is considered "an approximation of insight." Therefore, it is not the case that one first attains true insight and then later, after much more practice, unites it with serenity. Tsong-kha-pa says, "From the time that you first attain insight, you will have that union." Analytical wisdom is true insight when, within that very session of meditation, analysis induces and becomes fused with serenity.

While our concern here is analysis of the *ultimate* nature of phenomena and serenity focused upon that, it is worth noting that serenity and insight each may be focused on either the ultimate nature of all phenomena (emptiness) or on some conventional object of meditation. The term "insight" can sometimes refer to analytical wisdom discerning a conventional object, such as impermanence, as long as that wisdom is able to induce serene concentration upon that object.

The attainment of insight into emptiness is a crucial step forward on the path. This locks in one's cognition of ultimate reality by linking it to the supernormal power of meditative serenity. Nonetheless, even at this point, insight is a conceptual knowledge of emptiness. It is dualistic in the sense that the mind apprehends and focuses upon an image or idea of emptiness. At this point, the bodhisattva knows emptiness through the medium of that mental representation. Can a conceptual understanding of something, however profound, set the stage for a nondualistic perception of that same object?

One of Tsong-kha-pa's key messages in the *Great Treatise* is that the answer to this question is, "Yes, absolutely, if you know what you are doing. Moreover, it is *only* by starting out with conceptual analysis that you have *any* chance of coming to know the ultimate reality in a direct, nondualistic manner." In support of this, Tsong-kha-pa quotes the Buddha, who—in the *Kashyapa Chapter Sutra*—teaches,

> Kashyapa, it is like this. For example, two trees are dragged against each other by wind and from that a fire starts, burning the two trees. In the same way, Kashyapa, if you have correct analytical discrimination, the power of a noble being's wisdom will emerge. With its emergence, correct analytical discrimination will itself be burned up.

In other words, powerful and correct analysis of emptiness, while conceptual and dualistic, gives rise to the ultimate mind—nonconceptual, direct perception of emptiness. Such direct realization is utterly nondualistic. In the fire of this wisdom, all of the dualism of the original analysis is burned away.

Some may object that this is a contradiction because there is a lack of harmony between the cause—dualistic analysis—and the effect—nondual wisdom. Tsong-kha-pa points out that causes are often quite different from their effects. Fire is unlike smoke. A grey seed is unlike a green sprout. In this case, there is a great harmony between cause and effect in the sense that both are forms of wisdom knowing the emptiness of intrinsic nature.

To reinforce his point, Tsong-kha-pa returns to cite a passage from the *King of Concentrations Sutra*. In a sense, the entirety of the

Great Treatise's insight section can be seen as an elaboration of this striking bit of scripture:[10]

> If you analytically discern the lack of self in phenomena
> And if you cultivate that very analysis in meditation,
> This will cause the result, attainment of nirvana;
> There is no peace through any other means.

A Complete Practice

In this book we have explained in a modest way some of what Tsong-kha-pa teaches in the insight section of the *Great Treatise*. Considering just these things gives one a good start at understanding Tsong-kha-pa's ideas about meditation on emptiness, but it distorts the total message of Tsong-kha-pa's teaching. An absolutely crucial point for Tsong-kha-pa—a point that underlies the entire conception and design of the *Great Treatise*—is that one should not rush to what one thinks of as "higher" practices, neglecting basic trainings that are the foundation of the path. As Tsong-kha-pa puts it,

> Some say to expend your energy only to stabilize your mind and to understand the view, ignoring all earlier topics, but this makes it very difficult to get the vital points. Therefore, you must develop certainty about the whole course of the path.

Tsong-kha-pa advises that everyone must proceed from the foundational practices to more advanced training. Also, as you train in new and higher practices, you must constantly "go back to balance your mind" by practicing earlier meditations again. Long after you have had success with basic practices, you should return to them so as to renew, sustain, and reinforce, for example, your faith in your spiritual teacher, your understanding of impermanence, karma, and mortality, your disenchantment with cyclic existence, your commitment to any vows you have taken, and your aspiration to enlightenment for the sake of helping all living beings.

Tsong-kha-pa concludes the *Great Treatise* by insisting that one must enter the Vajrayana path—which is to say, Buddhist tantric practice. However, this is to be done "after you have trained in the paths common to both sutra and mantra." In other words, all of the key elements of general Mahayana practice, as presented in the *Great Treatise* as a whole, are foundations without which one is not suited for the distinctive practices of tantra. Tsong-kha-pa teaches us that by entering and practicing Buddhist tantra on the basis of a proper foundation, we will make our lives worthwhile. We will bring happiness to all, extending the benefit of the Buddha's teaching both within our own minds and within the lives of others.

Appendix:
The Quintessential Points Chapter by Chapter

Chapter 1

▸ Happiness depends upon seeing our deep connections to other beings. We suffer unnecessarily because we have a persistent sense of ourselves as existing independently, by way of our own private essence.

▸ Emptiness is the utter nonexistence of any intrinsic nature or real essence. Emptiness does not mean nothingness or meaninglessness. It means that things exist *only* interdependently, lacking any independent nature.

▸ Knowing emptiness frees us. Our current limitations and faults are not locked into our nature; our minds are open even to radical transformation.

▸ The path to the perfect happiness of a buddha requires (1) wisdom understanding that there is no essential existence and (2) compassion seeking to free all beings from suffering. These two—caring for beings and seeing that all is empty—work synergistically to bring about enlightenment.

▸ Wisdom involves not only seeing the ultimate reality—emptiness—but also making careful distinctions at the conventional level about how best to practice, how best to help others.

▸ To develop profound wisdom knowing emptiness, first study scripture and carefully reflect upon its meaning—guided by a qualified teacher. Study is itself a form of practice. Meditation is deep familiarization with something one has studied and come to understand.

▸ Happiness flows from virtue; all virtue derives from reflecting on facts with an undistracted mind. Thus, the path to buddha-hood involves both stabilizing the mind in perfect nondistrac-tion and training in analysis that leads to meditative insight.

Chapter 2

▸ The path to enlightenment involves logically refuting in med-itation the sense of an essentially real self. Bodhisattvas then gradually strip away dualistic and conceptual aspects of this knowledge until they experience emptiness directly and non-dualistically.

▸ Of the three trainings on the Buddhist path—ethics, meditative stabilization, and wisdom—the first two are similar to many non-Buddhist teachings. What is unique in Buddhism is wis-dom, born of analytical meditation, which penetrates the nature of ultimate reality.

▸ To prepare for this, one must study and reflect on definitive scrip-tures such as the Perfection of Wisdom sutras that teach the final nature of reality as emptiness. To understand these texts, we can rely on Madhyamika interpreters such as Nagarjuna, Aryadeva, Buddhapalita, Chandrakirti, and Shantideva.

▸ Wisdom eradicates the ignorance or delusion that is the root of all misery. This ignorance is a mind that superimposes intrinsic nature, when in fact all things are devoid of such. This "intrinsic nature" or "essential nature" is also sometimes called "self."

▸ The utter lack of intrinsic nature in persons is "the selflessness of persons"; the utter lack of intrinsic nature in other phenomena is "the selflessness of phenomena." Neither selflessness is more profound; they are the same quality, emptiness, considered in relation to different things.

Chapter 3

▸ It is not enough to withdraw the mind from mistaken ideas by placing it in a thoughtless condition. This leaves the roots of ignorance intact. It is necessary to introspectively identify the conception of an essential self and then to use analysis to refute it.

▸ It is vital to identify very precisely just how ignorance misapprehends things so that we refute neither too little nor too much. Refuting too much undermines ethics and leads to nihilism.

▸ Madhyamaka, the middle way, teaches that dependent arising and emptiness are fully compatible. Within utter emptiness, effects arise from their respective causes and conditions.

▸ A reflection of a face falsely appears to be a face but nonetheless exists, arises from conditions, and produces effects. Analogously, tables, chairs, persons, etc. falsely appear to exist by way of their own intrinsic natures, but nonetheless they do exist and function conventionally.

Chapter 4

▸ There is nothing that can bear ultimate analysis. Everything, when interrogated as to the ultimate conditions of its nature, is found to be empty.

▸ However, this analysis does not refute things. Not finding things under ultimate analysis means that they lack any ultimate or essential nature such as would be found under such analysis. Things exist only conventionally—which means that they *do* exist.

▸ Just as we do not see sounds no matter how carefully we look, objects exist conventionally even though not found under ultimate analysis. Like seeing and hearing, or like two different radio channels, conventional knowledge and ultimate knowledge are distinct and valid ways to get useful information about the world.

▸ Both kinds of knowledge are necessary on the path: ultimate knowledge gets at emptiness, thereby making it possible to escape cyclic existence; conventional knowledge differentiates right and wrong and allows compassion for conventionally existing persons.

▸ Nothing exists ultimately because all things lack any essential nature that would be findable under ultimate analysis. All things, even emptiness, exist only conventionally.

▸ Existing conventionally means (1) being known to a conventional consciousness, (2) not being contradicted by conventional knowledge, and (3) not being contradicted by ultimate knowledge.

▸ Examples: A table appears to a conventional mind, is established as a table by conventional knowledge, and still exists even though found to be empty by ultimate knowledge. A reflection's being a face appears to a conventional mind but is contradicted by conventional knowledge. The person having an essential self appears to a conventional mind, is not contradicted by conventional knowledge, but is contradicted by ultimate knowledge.

Chapter 5

▸ Our senses are deceived about *how* things exist. Things appear to them as though they were essentially real, objectively and independently established, when in fact they are not.

▸ Nonetheless, our senses are reliable sources of knowledge about what things exist when they are not impaired by echoes, optical illusions, disease, drugs, etc. A table falsely appears as though intrinsically real, yet nonetheless there is a table, and we know this through using our senses.

▸ Nothing exists, even conventionally, in the exaggerated way that things falsely appear to our senses.

▸ If the world actually existed in the solid way it appears to our senses, then the production from causes and conditions would have to involve a real thing's being produced from itself, from something else, from both, or from neither. Yet none of these alternatives works.

▸ This does not refute production from conditions; it does not refute dependent arising. This refutes the false appearance of production and so forth as intrinsically real. It refutes that kind of existence our senses present to us and which we habitually take for granted.

▸ Nagarjuna relentlessly attacks the distorted way that ignorance views things. Tsong-kha-pa fully accepts Nagarjuna's view. Responding to the need of his day, Tsong-kha-pa reframes it so as to emphasize the need to penetrate emptiness without falling into nihilism.

Chapter 6

▸ Emptiness exists. Emptiness is a sheer lack or absence, the absence of intrinsic nature. Inconceivably vast harm arises from the mistaken idea that intrinsic nature exists, so the utter absence of such a nature is extremely important.

▸ Emptiness is also the ultimate reality. When we ask of anything, "What is it *really*?" what we come to know at the end of our search is just emptiness.

▸ Ultimate wisdom knows emptiness, but emptiness exists only conventionally. When we ask about the essential nature of emptiness, we find that it is itself empty of any graspable nature. Nagarjuna's teaching that we should hold no dogmatic view about emptiness means that we should not view emptiness as intrinsically real.

▸ The word "nature" can refer to (1) the conventional nature of fire as hot, (2) the ignorance-imputed essential nature of things, or (3) the ultimate nature of things as empty. When Nagarjuna comments that "nature" means something that is not fabricated and does not depend upon something else, Chandrakirti takes this to refer to the ultimate nature. Things cannot be nonempty; they do not become empty at a particular time; they are necessarily and always empty.

▸ Thus emptiness does not depend on causes and conditions but still exists only conventionally, as a dependent arising. To say that it exists, there must be a mind that knows about it and makes the designation, "Emptiness exists."

‣ Tsong-kha-pa criticizes "emptiness-of-other" views in which liberation is attained through meditation on a real ultimate reality that is empty of conventional things but which is not empty of its own nature. Liberation is attained only through realizing that all existents are devoid of any real or intrinsic nature.

Chapter 7

‣ That things change implies that they are empty of existing by way of an intrinsic nature. However, impermanence is not the same as emptiness. If we refute only the idea of permanence, we have not refuted enough to realize emptiness.

‣ Being empty, all things exist only as dependent arisings. Things are dependent arisings in part because they exist only in dependence upon conceptual designation. This particular sense of dependent arising is very important in Madhyamaka.

‣ The ignorance that is at the root of suffering conceives of things as having their own way of existing without depending on being posited through the force of consciousness. To have such a way of existing is to have intrinsic nature.

‣ Examples like the letter A and the conventional nature of money help show how things can be merely conventional yet fully functional. Tsong-kha-pa argues that *all* things are like this. When we set aside how they appear to this or that consciousness and ask how they are in and of themselves, there is nothing we can point out.

‣ Things depend upon subject/object relationships, but this does not mean that whatever we imagine is real. On account of dreams, impaired vision, and so forth we mistakenly perceive things that do not exist at all.

‣ Different kinds of beings (gods, humans, ghosts, animals) may have different but equally correct perceptions of what is present at a certain time and place. This is possible because things have no independent, objective existence.

Chapter 8

▸ Tsong-kha-pa divides Madhyamaka into Chandrakirti's Prasangika and Bhavaviveka's Svatantrika. He finds Chandrakirti to have the correct view.

▸ All Madhyamikas accept that all things are empty in the sense that nothing withstands ultimate analysis—all things are ultimately empty. However, Svatantrika Madhyamikas accept that things have intrinsic nature, such as appears to our senses, conventionally. Prasangikas assert that if things had intrinsic nature at all, it would have to be found under ultimate analysis. Since it is not, all things lack intrinsic nature even conventionally.

▸ This philosophical difference is not immediately evident in the Indian texts. Tsong-kha-pa infers it from a close reading of Buddhapalita, Bhavaviveka, and Chandrakirti, especially their debates about how best to frame Madhyamaka arguments so as to help other people realize emptiness.

▸ Bhavaviveka insists that arguments must be framed as classic syllogisms that require a commonly appearing topic of debate. Since the opponent assumes that things have intrinsic nature, this implies that Bhavaviveka also accepts intrinsic nature at the conventional level.

▸ Chandrakirti prefers *reductio ad absurdum* arguments that draw out the internal contradictions of the opponent's view. This shows that he does not believe there are commonly appearing objects about which to debate with realists. This is because he rejects even the conventional existence of the intrinsic nature that appears to our senses.

▸ The preference for the *reductio* when debating with non-Madhyamikas does not mean that Prasangikas have no view or no position. They hold the view that all things are empty of intrinsic nature, and they will assert this view in syllogisms with opponents who are prepared, via prior argumentation, to benefit from it.

Chapter 9

▸ Madhyamaka analyses that refute self, or intrinsic nature, proceed by first identifying the "self" that will be the object of negation, then setting out a comprehensive list of ways such a self could exist, and then refuting in turn each of these ways.

▸ Tsong-kha-pa presents "the lack of sameness or difference" as an example of such reasoning, applying it first to a chariot and then to the person. If a chariot had intrinsic nature, thus existing in accordance with the way it appears to us, it would have to be the same as or intrinsically different from its parts.

▸ A chariot cannot be identical to its parts because it is single and they are plural and also because we say that it *has* its parts. Can the possessing agent *be* the object possessed? But it cannot be intrinsically different from them, for then it could be observed apart from them just as we can see horses and cows separately.

▸ Since the same kind of analysis applies to the person, the person does not intrinsically exist. However, the person does exist nominally, conventionally, as a dependent arising. Each person is unique and can act effectively, but this power does not arise from a private core or essence. Persons exist and can act only in dependence upon a web of shifting conditions. This is possible only because they are empty of any fixed nature.

▸ Meditating, including meditative reasoning, often produces altered states of consciousness in which appearances seem to shimmer. However, actual understanding of the illusion-like nature of things arises only when one knows emptiness and sees that it is just these empty persons who engage in actions and experience effects.

Chapter 10

▸ Nirvana is attained only by first discerning the lack of self and then cultivating that analysis in meditation. It will not help to withdraw the mind into a nonconceptual state where one is temporarily free from manifest forms of ignorance.

▸ Discursive analysis getting at emptiness is preliminary to and quite different from nondualistic nirvana. The way to bridge the gap is to combine the discerning power of analytic wisdom with the stability and focus of serenity.

▸ Serenity means that the mind and body have become pliant—serviceable and responsive—as the mind focuses one-pointedly and with perfect clarity upon an object. It is developed through practicing mindful attention to a chosen object within vigilance about distraction or even subtle slippage in the stability and clarity of the mind.

▸ Having first separately developed both serenity and discernment of emptiness, bodhisattvas alternate between (1) periods of stabilizing the mind in serenity focused on emptiness and (2) periods of refreshing a sharp discernment of emptiness through further discursive analysis.

▸ When analysis itself spontaneously induces serenity, this wisdom in which the powers of discernment and serenity are fused is called *insight*. Insight is a fully empowered and activated analytical mind, penetrating its object with steady and laserlike focus.

▸ Insight is still conceptual knowledge of emptiness because it is mediated by an image-idea of emptiness that appears to the mind. However, because the mind deeply penetrates ultimate reality and remains stable and clear, this practice leads to the nondualistic realization of nirvana.

▸ Meditation on emptiness needs to be combined with many other practices in order to lay a proper foundation for entering into the practice of tantra, or Vajrayana.

Glossary of Terms and Names¹¹

affliction (*nyon mongs*) — an aspect of consciousness that binds living beings to cyclic existence; for example, greed, hatred, delusion, fear, pride, envy.

aggregate (*phung po*) — the five aggregates are the mental and physical components of a living being: form, feeling, discrimination, compositional factors, and consciousness.

analysis (*dpyad pa*) — using reason to inquire into and seek deeper understanding of an object.

analytical meditation (*dpyad sgom*) — meditation using reason to seek deeper understanding of an object.

Aryadeva — Indian scholar and author of Madhyamaka treatises; an early follower of Nagarjuna who is identified as his spiritual son.

autonomous syllogism (*rang rgyud*) — a syllogism in which each part is established by the same type of valid knowledge for both the person advancing the argument and the person to whom it is advanced. This is possible because both recognize the intrinsic nature of the objects involved.

basis (*gzhi*) — all existing things, conventional and ultimate. These things are the "basis" for the practice of a spiritual path (*lam*) leading to the fruit (*'bras*) that is enlightenment.

Bhavaviveka — Indian scholar and author of Madhyamaka treatises. Known as a brilliant and scrupulous logician, his critique of Buddhapalita's reading of Nagarjuna is the basis of the Svatantrika system.

bodhisattva (*byang chub sems dpa'*) — a person on the path to becoming a fully enlightened buddha. In particular, a person who is confirmed in the spirit of enlightenment, the aspiration to become a buddha in order to be in the best possible situation to help all living beings.

buddha (*sangs rgyas*) — in this book refers to any buddha superior, that is, any person who has attained perfect and complete enlightenment on the Mahayana Buddhist path. The phrase "the Buddha" refers specifically to one buddha in particular—Shakyamuni Buddha, the historical founder of Buddhism.

Buddhapalita — author of an important early Indian commentary on Nagarjuna's *Fundamental Treatise*. Retrospectively characterized as a Prasangika Madhyamika.

Chandrakirti — Indian author of many important Madhyamaka texts, including a commentary on Nagarjuna's *Fundamental Treatise* in which he defends Buddhapalita against Bhavaviveka, thereby beginning the Prasangika tradition.

compassion (*snying rje*) — the wish that other living beings be free from suffering and the causes of suffering.

concentration (*ting nge 'dzin*) — a virtuous consciousness that stays fixed on its object of meditation without distraction to other things.

conceptual image (*don spyi*) — an internal mental object that represents what we are thinking about. For example, the general idea / image of ice cream that arises in my mind when I hear and understand the word "ice cream."

conceptual thought (*rtog pa*) — a consciousness that gets at its object via an internal mental image that represents the object in a general way; as distinct from perception, a consciousness to which an object directly appears.

consciousness (*shes pa*) — that which is clear and knowing. The subjective experience of any object; a synonym of awareness (*sems*) and mind (*blo*).

consequence (*thal 'gyur*) — an argument framed in the form, "It follows that X because of Y." Often used to pose contradictory consequences to an opponent, wherein the reason, Y, is something the opponent accepts and what follows from it, X, is something absurd or contrary to the opponent's position.

conventional truth (*kun rdzob bden pa*) — objects found by conventional minds that are not analyzing the ultimate nature of things. This includes everything that exists except emptiness. Nonexistents are not included.

cyclic existence (*'khor pa, srid pa*) — the condition of all living beings who have not attained liberation. We are trapped in a beginningless cycle of birth, death, and rebirth on the basis of our actions and afflictions.

dependent arising (*rten 'byung*) — the core teaching that "in dependence upon this, that arises," which is the heart of the Dharma. Since there is nothing that exists in and of itself, all existents are dependent arisings. One important case of dependent arising is the arising of cyclic existence in dependence upon ignorance, karma, and other linked conditions.

Dharma (*chos*) — what the Buddha taught. Includes all teachings, but since the Buddha taught the reality and truth of things, sometimes used specifically in the sense of the ultimate reality.

discursive mind (*rtog pa*) — a thinking mind; that is, a conceptual consciousness in which the mind is not fixed one-pointedly, but is fluctuating or moving from object to object. According to context, the same Tibetan term can also mean any conceptual consciousness even though not all conceptual consciousnesses are discursive. For example, serenity focused on emptiness, prior to attainment of nirvana, is conceptual but nondiscursive.

embodiment of form (*gzugs sku*) — the aspect of a buddha's perfect enlightenment that arises from the imprint of the vast accumulation of merit on the bodhisattva path.

embodiment of truth (*chos sku*) — the aspect of a buddha's perfect enlightenment that arises from the imprint of the vast accumulation of wisdom on the bodhisattva path.

emptiness (*stong pa nyid*) — the sheer nonexistence of intrinsic nature. For example, the table's emptiness is the table's lack of existence by way of an intrinsic nature.

enlightenment (*byang chub*) — the completion of a Buddhist spiritual path in a condition of profound awakening. The buddhas, having completed the Mahayana path, have attained the state of perfect and complete enlightenment.

essence (*rang gi ngo bo nyid*) — "own being" or intrinsic identity. Emptiness means that things lack any kind of existence on the basis of an essential or intrinsic nature.

fruit (*'bras*) — what is attained as the final culmination of a spiritual path (*lam*). The fruit of the Mahayana path is perfect and complete enlightenment as a buddha.

Ge-luk (*dge lugs*) — the "order of virtue," the Tibetan Buddhist tradition established by Tsong-kha-pa and including the Dalai Lamas.

Ha-shang Mahayana — a Chinese teacher who functions in the *Great Treatise* as a stock character representing the teaching that one must engage ultimate reality by holding the mind without any thought whatsoever.

Hinayana (*theg dman*) — a Buddhist path that is based upon seeking liberation for oneself rather than upon an aspiration to attain buddhahood for the sake of all; also, philosophical systems associated with that path.

ignorance (*ma rig pa*) — a wrong conception or delusion; often used in reference to a false conception that something has intrinsic nature.

illusory (*sgyu ma lta bu*) — things appearing to the mind, but not existing objectively—in and of themselves. When one rises from meditation on emptiness, one may have the experience of recognizing the illusory nature of things.

impermanence (*mi rtag pa*) — the quality of changing instant by instant; also, the more obvious quality of existing in such a manner as to fall apart sooner or later.

inherent existence (*rang gi mtshan nyid gyi grub pa*) — the existence of something by the power of its own intrinsic or essential character.

insight (*lhag mthong*) — analytical wisdom that directly induces and becomes fused with meditative serenity.

intrinsic nature (*rang bzhin*) — an essential nature whereby something comes to have an independent way of existing without being posited through the force of consciousness. The sheer absence of this is emptiness.

Kamalashila — a Svatantrika Madhyamaka scholar from India who, according to Tibetan tradition, established Indian Buddhism as the model for Tibet by defeating Ha-shang in debate.

karma (*las*) — the actions that we choose; also, the conditioning power of the actions we have chosen in the past.

lack of sameness and difference (*gcig du bral*) — the argument that something does not intrinsically exist because it is neither identical to nor intrinsically different from its parts.

latent predispositions (*bag chags*) — nonmanifest forms of afflictions. Like seeds left behind by earlier weeds, they embody the potential for afflictions to become manifest again.

liberation (*thar pa*) — the culmination of a spiritual path in freedom from cyclic existence.

logic (*tog ge*) — a formal system for the formulation and evaluation of reasoned arguments.

Madhyamaka (*dbu ma*) — the Mahayana philosophical tradition, pioneered by Nagarjuna, in which nothing whatsoever exists in an ultimate sense.

Mahayana (*theg chen*) — a Buddhist path based on the spirit of enlightenment, the aspiration to attain buddhahood for the sake of all living beings; also, philosophical systems associated with this path.

meditative stabilization (*bsam gtan*) — virtuous consciousness that stays fixed on its object of meditation without distraction to other things.

merit (*bsod nams*) — the potency of past virtuous actions.

mind (*blo*) — not the container of consciousness, but a synonym of awareness (*sems*) and consciousness (*shes pa*). The subjective experience of any object.

mindfulness (*dran pa*) — not forgetting the object you are attending to; specifically, mental focus that is characterized by not being distracted from the object upon which one is meditating.

mistaken consciousness (*'khrul shes*) — a consciousness that gets at its object via an erroneous appearance. In Prasangika Madhyamaka, only minds realizing emptiness are utterly nonmistaken. Mistaken consciousness can be right or wrong about their main object; also, they can be either conceptual or nonconceptual.

Nagarjuna — author of the *Fundamental Treatise on Wisdom* and many other classic treatises; the founder of the Madhyamaka system.

nature (*rang bzhin*) — may refer to (1) a conventional quality of an existent, such as the heat of fire; (2) an intrinsic nature whereby something exists on its own power; or (3) the final nature of all things, their emptiness of intrinsic nature.

nirvana (*myang ngan las 'das pa*) — the utter dissolution into emptiness of at least one portion of the afflictions, including the dissolution of all predispositions for that portion ever to arise again in one's mind-stream.

path (*lam*) — a state of consciousness that is part of a practice leading to liberation; loosely but commonly used to refer to the progressive sequence of such consciousnesses.

perfections (*pha rol tu phyin pa*) — virtues practiced on the bodhisattva path.

pliancy (*shin sbyangs*) — serviceability, or responsiveness, of mind or body as developed in the practice of meditation.

Prasangika (*thal 'gyur pa*) — the Madhyamaka system of Chandrakirti and his followers, characterized by the refutation of intrinsic nature even conventionally. Also, any person who follows this system not in a vague way, but on the basis of definitely knowing it.

realist (*dngos por smra ba*) — one holding the view that some or all existents are possessed of ultimate existence, meaning that they can be analytically located by a mind searching out their true nature.

reality (*de kho na nyid, chos nyid, de bzhin nyid*) — synonym for emptiness, the ultimate truth.

reasoning (*rig pa*) — an argument used to bring about inferential knowledge; the general process of constructing and using such arguments.

reductio ad absurdum (*'gal ba'i thal 'gyur*) — an argument in which the thesis is absurd but follows logically from a reason that the other person accepts.

samsara (*'khor ba, srid pa*) — the beginningless cycle of suffering in which living beings are trapped because of their karma and afflictions.

self (*bdag*) — sometimes refers to the person—that is, to something that does conventionally exist. However, often refers to a reified nature that does not exist at all but is wrongly superimposed on persons and other things.

selflessness (*bdag med pa*) — the nonexistence of a reified nature that ignorance wrongly superimposes on persons and other things. In Prasangika Madhyamaka, the nonexistence of intrinsic nature in a person or other existing things.

serenity (*zhi gnas*) — a mental state characterized by extremely clear, one-pointed attention to a single object and subtle pliancy of the mind and body.

Shantarakshita — a Svatantrika Madhyamika who, unlike Bhavaviveka, was influenced by Buddhist idealism and held that there are no objects external to mind.

Shay-rap-gyal-tsen (*shes rab rgyal mtshan*) — a highly influential fourteenth-century Tibetan teacher of the doctrine of "other-emptiness," the view that emptiness is not things' lack of their own intrinsic nature, but their lack of being the ultimate.

spiritual teacher (*bla ma*) — a person upon whom a practitioner relies for guidance in the practice of the path.

stabilizing meditation (*'jog sgom*) — meditation seeking to establish or reestablish the mind in a state of steady, one-pointed attention.

sutra (*mdo*) — a nontantric scripture regarded as the word of the Buddha.

Svatantrika (*rang rgyud pa*) — the Madhyamaka tradition beginning in the work of Bhavaviveka, characterized (according to Tsong-kha-pa) by the view that nothing exists ultimately, but things do have intrinsic nature conventionally.

syllogism (*'byor ba*) — an argument in the form "As to X, Y is the case because of Z; as in the case of Q." For example, "My body is impermanent because it is produced from causes and conditions, just like the morning dew."

tantra (*rguyd*) — Vajrayana, or scriptures of Vajrayana.

tetralemma — a four-pronged argument refuting ultimately existing production of any existent.

ultimate mind (*don dam pa'i blo*) — a consciousness discerning the final nature of an object.

ultimate truth (*don dam bden pa*) — the object known by a mind discerning the final nature of things—emptiness.

union of serenity and insight (*zhi lhag zung 'brel*) — a meditative state in which analytical wisdom directly induces and becomes fused with serenity.

Vajrayana (*rdo rje'i theg pa*) — the path of esoteric Buddhism, in which, under the direction of a qualified spiritual teacher, one learns to practice deity yoga—that is, visualizing with conviction that one's body, speech, mind, environment, and companions are those of a fully enlightened buddha.

valid (*tshad ma*) — reliable, authoritative. In this book, used in reference to consciousnesses in which the primary cognition is definitively right.

view (*lta ba*) — philosophical conclusion. Tsong-kha-pa often uses this as shorthand for "the correct view" (*yang dag pa'i lta ba*), that is, the position that all things are empty.

view of the perishing aggregates (*'jig tshog lta ba*) — a type of ignorant mind, or wrong consciousness, that views one's own person as intrinsically existent. The root cause of cyclic existence.

vigilance (*shes bzhin*) — a mind that accurately monitors whether laxity or excitement is present as one is practicing stabilizing meditation. For example, it includes the quality of mind that allows you to notice when you are becoming distracted from your object of meditation.

virtue (*dge ba*) — that which creates the conditions for future happiness.

wisdom (*shes rab*) — correct, discerning knowledge of ultimate or conventional truths.

wrong consciousness (*log shes*) — A mind that is wrong about its main object; for example, the thought that there are two moons in the sky when there is one.

Suggested Reading

I highly recommend His Holiness the Dalai Lama's *How to See Yourself As You Really Are* (Atria Books, 2006). This is a very clear summary of how to meditate on emptiness.

The present volume is mainly based upon the insight section (within Volume Three) of Tsong-kha-pa's *The Great Treatise on the Stages of the Path to Enlightenment* (Snow Lion Publications, 2000–2004). I hope you will use my book to begin working your way into Tsong-kha-pa's teachings on the path.

For expert traditional commentary on Tsong-kha-pa's *Great Treatise*, see the *Steps on the Path to Enlightenment* series by Geshe Sopa (Wisdom Publications, 2004–). The series has not yet reached the section on emptiness.

Elizabeth Napper's *Dependent-Arising and Emptiness* (Wisdom Publications, 1989) includes an earlier translation and clear explanation of a large and important portion of what appears in Volume Three of the *Great Treatise*.

Two books that I read when I began studying are available in reissued editions and are still great places to start: Kensur Lekden's *Meditations of a Tibetan Tantric Abbot* (Snow Lion Publications, 2001) and Sopa and Hopkins's *Cutting Through Appearances* (Snow Lion Publications, 1990).

In addition to *How to See Yourself As You Really Are*, at least three other recent books by the Dalai Lama deal directly with emptiness:

How to Practice (Pocket Books, 2003) is a very basic introduction; *Essence of the Heart Sutra* (Wisdom Publications, 2006) explains this famous scripture; and *Practicing Wisdom* (Wisdom Publications, 2005) explains the Wisdom Chapter of Shantideva's *The Way of the Bodhisattva.*

Gen Lamrimpa lays out the practice of using Madhyamaka reasoning to see reality in *Realizing Emptiness* (Snow Lion Publications, 1999).

Contemplating Reality (Shambhala, 2007) by Andy Karr is a witty, well-written book that shows us how another tradition within Tibetan Buddhism looks at some of the same issues presented here.

Tsong-kha-pa's *Ocean of Reasoning*, translated by Geshe Ngawang Samten and Jay Garfield (Oxford University Press, 2006), is his detailed commentary on the most important Indian Madhyamaka text, Nagarjuna's *Fundamental Wisdom.*

Jeffrey Hopkins's *Meditation on Emptiness* (Wisdom Publications, 1983) is the classic, comprehensive, and authoritative work on this topic. You won't be reading it in one sitting, but you will keep going back to it for years. Hopkins's *Emptiness Yoga* (Snow Lion Publications, 1987) uses a more personal voice, coaching us through painstaking analysis of how our ordinary way of perceiving the world is wrong.

Some readers have found helpful my *Appearance and Reality* (Snow Lion Publications, 1999), which examines how Tsong-kha-pa's Ge-luk tradition understands the relationship between the ultimate and the conventional. In *The Two Truths* (Snow Lion Publications, 1992), I scrutinize the efforts of Ge-luk scholars to work out some of the finer points of Madhyamaka philosophy.

Notes

1 The scriptural basis for this example is found in *The Condensed Perfection of Wisdom Sutra*, which teaches:

> Investigate the example of how one sees space
> In living beings' verbal expression of the words "seeing space."
> In this way also the Tathagata teaches seeing Dharma.
> Other examples cannot convey the meaning of this seeing.

In ordinary parlance, the nonseeing of obstructive contact is called "seeing space." Analogously, the nonseeing of form in the perspective of an ultimate mind searching for that object among its bases of designation is called "seeing the emptiness of form."

The sutra citation in this note is my translation of the passage as it appears within Jam-yang-shay-ba's *Great Exposition of the Middle Way* (*Collected Works of Jam dbyang bshad pa*, vol. 9, 579 [New Delhi: Ngawang Gelek Demo, 1972]).

2 Based loosely on Hopkins's *Meditation on Emptiness* (Wisdom Publications, 1983), 545–547, which includes a vivid excerpt from Den-dar-hla-ram-ba's *Presentation of the Lack of Being One or Many* in his *Collected Works*, vol. 1 (New Delhi: Lama Guru Deva, 1971), 425.1ff.

3 My comment here is based on Geshe Rabten's commentary on the *Heart Sutra*, as excerpted in Jean Smith, ed., *Radiant Mind* (Riverhead Books, 1999), 183.

4 David S. Ruegg, *The Literature of the Madhyamaka School of Philosophy in India* (Otto Harrassowitz, 1981), 2–3.

5 The "A" example is adapted from Jeffrey Hopkins, *The Tantric Distinction* (Wisdom Publications, 1984), 16–18. It seems likely that some of the other examples in this book are things I have appropriated and internalized after hearing them from Jeffrey.

6 This paragraph is inspired by Geshe Rabten, *Song of the Profound View* (Wisdom Publications, 1989), which consists of short verses and an autocommentary on his experiences with emptiness before, during, and after an extended meditation retreat. I value this text because of its deeply personal descriptions, honestly expressing doubts as well as insights. Rabten (48) explains that his meditative investigations of emptiness began when he was "greatly moved" by his teacher's use of a one-hundred-rupee note to explain the imputed nature of all phenomena.

7   From Chapter Two of *Alice's Adventures in Wonderland* by Lewis Carroll. Modern Library (2002) has a nice edition.

8   Adapted from Jeffrey Hopkins, *Emptiness Yoga* (Snow Lion Publications, 1987), 207.

9   Elsewhere, Tsong-kha-pa uses the excluded middle (*Great Treatise*, Volume 3: 146–147) and backs it up with a citation from Nagarjuna: "Limiting things to two possibilities—either they intrinsically exist or they do not—derives from the universal limitation that anything imaginable either exists or does not exist. Similarly, the limitation that what truly exists must either truly exist as single or truly exist as plural is based on the universal limitation that anything must be either single or plural. When there is such a limitation, any further alternative is necessarily precluded; hence, it is utter nonsense to assert a phenomenon that is neither of those two. As Nagarjuna's *Vigrahavyavartani* says:

> If the absence of intrinsic existence were overturned,
> Intrinsic existence would be established.

10 The *Great Treatise* cites this verse three times: at the opening of the serenity section (Volume 3: 27) and then at the beginning and end of the insight section (Volume 3: 108 and 345). In this book, I first cited this verse on p. 102.

11 I offer these glosses to help readers find their way, not for the purpose of scholarly debate. Some are formulated based on definitions used in Geluk scholasticism, but most are worded so as to be informative rather than definitive.